In Praise of *The Untethered Soul*

"In the book *The Untethered Soul*, Michael Singer takes you step-by-step through the process of Gyana, the yoga of the Intellect, to the Source. Moreover, he does it with elegant simplicity. Read this book carefully, and you will get more than a glimpse of eternity."

—**Deepak Chopra**, author of *Life After Death: The Burden of Proof*

"*The Untethered Soul* is indeed one of the finest treatments of the nature and practice of the conscious use of consciousness that I have ever read… It is the clearest statement I know, of who we are and what we face in our emerging humanity."

—**Jean Houston**, philosopher, psychologist, and author of *A Mythic Life* and *Passion for the Possible*

"Michael Singer has opened my mind to an entirely new dimension of thought. Through *The Untethered Soul,* I have been challenged both psychologically and intellectually in a new and exciting way. It may take more than one reading and many hours of introspection, but *The Untethered Soul* is a must-read for anyone in search of greater understanding of themselves and of the truth."

—**Louis Chiavacci**, senior vice-president of Merrill Lynch, ranked in Barron's top fifteen US Investment Advisors

"*The Untethered Soul* is a brilliant treatment of the path of spiritual consciousness. It is clearly and powerfully written. Michael Singer provides a firm step for those on a spiritual journey."

—**Abdul Aziz Said**, professor of Peace Studies and chair of Islamic Peace at American University

"This publication has released boundless joy for the hungry souls of the world."

—**Ma Yoga Shakti Saraswati,** founder of Yogashakti International Mission and recipient of *Hinduism Today's* "Hindu of the Year 2000" award

"Psalm 42:8 says, 'Deep calls unto deep.' Within each human soul there is a longing for more, and the thirst can be quenched only by God. In *The Untethered Soul*, Michael Singer helps the modern person who is seeking this experience to come to a better understanding of the action in their soul. I highly recommend this reflection of one soul to another on the journey."

—**Fr. Paul Wierichs, CP**, director of the Passionist Monastery and Spiritual Center of Our Lady of Florida

"This is a seminal book that quite frankly is in a class by itself. In a simple, yet paradoxically profound way, Michael Singer takes the reader on a journey that begins with consciousness tethered to the ego and ends having taken us beyond our myopic, contained self-image to a state of inner freedom and liberation. Michael Singer's book is a priceless gift to all who have futilely searched and yearned for a richer, more meaningful, creative life."

—**Yogi Amrit Desai**, internationally recognized pioneer of modern yoga

the untethered soul

the journey beyond yourself

MICHAEL A. SINGER

Noetic Books, Institute of Noetic Sciences
New Harbinger Publications, Inc.

Publisher's Note

A copublication of New Harbinger Publications and Noetic Books.

The Untethered Soul is a registered trademark of Shanti Publications, Inc.

Distributed in Canada by Raincoast Books

New Harbinger Publications, Inc.
5674 Shattuck Avenue
Oakland, CA 94609
www.newharbinger.com

Acquired by Catharine Meyers

Library of Congress has the paperback edition cataloged as:

Singer, Michael A.
  The untethered soul : the journey beyond yourself / Michael A. Singer.
     p. cm.
  ISBN-13: 978-1-57224-537-2
  ISBN-10: 1-57224-537-9
  1. Consciousness. 2. Self. I. Title.
  BF311.S5683 2007
  153--dc22

                        2007028150

Printed in the United States of America

23   22   21

15   14   13

To the Masters

contents

preface

When I sat down to write *The Untethered Soul*, the intention behind the book was very simple: I wanted to share a path to complete inner freedom with anyone willing to receive it. Spiritual growth should not be difficult or esoteric—it should be simple, clear, and intuitively obvious. Freedom is the most natural thing in the world—it is, in fact, our birthright. The problem is that we obscure this simple truth with our mind, emotions, and preferences. *The Untethered Soul* takes us on a journey in which we directly experience the innate truths within us. We discover who we are by letting go of who we are not. This deep inner journey is not intended just for mystics or scholars; it is a journey back to the seat of Self, and it can be taken by anyone.

The Untethered Soul

For the first six years after its publication, *The Untethered Soul* became very popular on its own, mostly through word of mouth. The feedback from everywhere was overwhelming. The book was fulfilling its purpose: it was helping people. Knowing that others are being helped is a great gift, especially when some have had no prior background or interest in spiritual growth. So many have shared how their lives have completely changed. Some have even described *The Untethered Soul* as a handbook for life that should be required reading for everyone on the planet. Many have reported that their concepts, habits, and deeply held fears no longer have a hold on them. They have tasted freedom and have no intention of looking back.

Upon completing the book in 2006, if I had been asked to voice my heartfelt wish for *The Untethered Soul*, it would have been that the book find its way around the globe to anyone who could be lifted by its message. Amazingly, that is exactly what happened. Publishers from all over the world began to request the rights to translate the book into their native languages. It started with Turkey, followed by Japan, China, and Denmark, to name just a few. Then came a great surprise—a wave of formerly Eastern Bloc countries like Hungary, Poland, Slovakia, and the Czech Republic began to publish the book. What a gift to know that *The Untethered Soul* could play its part in taking down the walls that stand between us as fellow human beings.

I was overwhelmed by the tremendous success of *The Untethered Soul.* But there was no way I could have known that I hadn't seen anything yet. In 2012, a friend of Oprah Winfrey's gave her *The Untethered Soul* as a birthday gift. Oprah loved the book and immediately set out to share it with others. It wasn't too long afterward that I was asked to do an interview with Oprah, which was quite an experience in and of itself. What an honor to meet such a beautiful soul with such a sincere wish to share inner freedom with others. The interview was first aired in August 2012, inviting a world of new readers to share the book with their family and friends.

How appropriate that a book that has been a gift to so many people in so many ways is now available in this beautiful gift edition. May *The Untethered Soul* bring you the great gift of freedom and happiness that it has brought so many others. In truth, that would be the greatest gift to me.

With great love and respect,

Michael A. Singer
August 2013

acknowledgments

The seeds for this work were planted many years ago when Linda Bean was transcribing some of my lectures and encouraged me to write a book. She patiently labored through years of archived material until it was time for me to begin writing. Her commitment and dedication to this project are deeply appreciated.

Once I began writing, Karen Entner assisted me by organizing materials, making content suggestions, and maintaining the manuscript. We worked together to edit version after version until the flow of words brought a sense of peace to the heart, mind, and soul. Her dedication and heartfelt work are much appreciated and one of her lifelong dreams comes to fruition with the publication of this book.

introduction

"This above all: to thine own self be true, and it must follow, as the night the day, thou canst not then be false to any man."
—William Shakespeare

The Untethered Soul

Shakespeare's age-honored words, spoken by Polonius to his son Laertes in Act I of Hamlet, sound so clear and unambiguous. They tell us that to maintain honest relations with others we must first be true to ourselves. Yet if Laertes were to be totally honest with himself, he would realize that his father may as well have told him to catch the wind. After all, to which "self" are we to be true? Is it the one that shows up when we're in a bad mood, or the one that is present when we feel humbled by our mistakes? Is it the one who speaks from the dark recesses of the heart when we're depressed or upset, or the one that appears during those fleeting moments when life seems so fanciful and light?

From these questions we see that the concept of "self" may turn out to be a bit more elusive than initially presumed. Perhaps if Laertes could have turned to traditional psychology, it would have shed some light on the subject. Freud (1927), the father of psychology, divided the psyche into three parts: the id, the ego, and the superego. He saw the id as our primal, animal nature; the superego as the judgment system that society has instilled within us; and the ego as our representative to the outside world that struggles to maintain a balance between the other two powerful forces. But this certainly would not have helped young Laertes. After all, to which of these conflicting forces are we to be true?

Introduction

Again we see that things are not always as simple as they seem. If we dare to look past the surface of the term "self," questions arise that many people would rather not ask: "Are the many aspects of my being all equally part of my 'self,' or is there only one of me—and if so, which, where, how, and why?"

In the following chapters, we will undertake a journey of exploration of "self." But we will not do so in a traditional manner. We will neither call upon the experts in psychology, nor upon the great philosophers. We will not argue and choose between time-honored religious views, or resort to statistically supported surveys of people's opinions. We will, instead, turn to a single source that has phenomenal direct knowledge on the subject. We will turn to one expert who, for every moment of every day of their life, has been collecting the data necessary to finally put this great inquiry to rest. And that expert is you.

But before you get too excited, or decide that you're not up to the task, first be clear that we're not after your views or opinions on the subject. Neither are we interested in what books you have read, classes you have taken, nor seminars you have attended. We are only interested in your intuitive experience of what it is like to be you. We are not looking for your knowledge; we are seeking your direct experience. You see, you can't fail at this because your "self" is what you are, at all times and in all places. We simply need to sort it out. After all, it can get quite confusing in there.

The chapters of this book are nothing but mirrors for seeing your "self" from different angles. And though the journey we are about to embark on is an inner one, it will draw upon every aspect of your life. The only requirement asked of you is the willingness to honestly look at yourself in the most natural, intuitive manner. Remember, if we are seeking the root of "self," what we are actually seeking is you.

As you read through these pages, you will find that you know much more than you thought you did about some very deep subjects. The fact is, you already know how to find yourself; you have just gotten distracted and disoriented. Once refocused, you will realize that you not only have the ability to find yourself, you have the ability to free yourself. Whether you choose to do so or not is entirely up to you. But upon completion of your journey through these chapters, there will be no more confusion, no more lack of empowerment, and no more blaming others. You will know exactly what must be done. And should you choose to devote yourself to the ongoing journey of self-realization, you will develop a tremendous sense of respect for who you really are. It is only then that you will come to appreciate the full depth of meaning in the advice: "This above all: to thine own self be true."

PART I

awakening consciousness

CHAPTER 1

the voice inside
your head

The Untethered Soul

"Shoot, I can't remember her name. What is her name? Darn, here she comes. What is it... Sally... Sue? She just told me yesterday. What's the matter with me? This is going to be embarrassing."

In case you haven't noticed, you have a mental dialogue going on inside your head that never stops. It just keeps going and going. Have you ever wondered why it talks in there? How does it decide what to say and when to say it? How much of what it says turns out to be true? How much of what it says is even important? And if right now you are hearing, "I don't know what you're talking about. I don't have any voice inside my head!"— that's the voice we're talking about.

If you're smart, you'll take the time to step back, examine this voice, and get to know it better. The problem is, you're too close to be objective. You have to step way back and watch it converse. While you're driving, you hear internal conversations like,

"Wasn't I supposed to call Fred? I should have. Oh my God, I can't believe I forgot! He's going to be so mad. He may never talk to me again. Maybe I should stop and call

him right now. No. I don't want to stop the
car right now…"

Notice that the voice takes both sides of the conversation. It doesn't care which side it takes, just as long as it gets to keep on talking. When you're tired and trying to sleep, it's the voice inside your head that says,

"What am I doing? I can't go to sleep yet. I
forgot to call Fred. I remembered in the car
but I didn't call. If I don't call now…oh wait,
it's too late. I shouldn't call him now. I don't
even know why I thought about it. I need to
fall asleep. Oh shoot, now I can't fall asleep.
I'm not tired anymore. But I have a big day
tomorrow, and I have to get up early."

No wonder you can't sleep! Why do you even tolerate that voice talking to you all the time? Even if what it's saying is soothing and nice, it's still disturbing everything you're doing.

If you spend some time observing this mental voice, the first thing you will notice is that it never shuts up. When left to its own, it just talks. Imagine if you were to see someone walking around constantly talking to himself. You'd think he was strange. You'd wonder, "If he's the one who's talking and he's the one who's listening, he obviously knows what's going to be said before he says it. So what's the point?" The same is true for the voice inside your head. Why is it talking? It's you who's talking, and it's you who's listening. And when the voice argues with itself, who is it arguing with? Who could possibly win? It gets very confusing. Just listen:

> "I think I should get married. No! You know you're not ready. You'll be sorry. But I love him. Oh come on, you felt that way about Tom. What if you had married him?"

If you watch carefully, you'll see that it's just trying to find a comfortable place to rest. It will change sides in a moment if that seems to help. And it doesn't even quiet down when it finds out that it's wrong. It simply adjusts its viewpoint and keeps on going. If you pay attention, these mental patterns will become obvious to you. It's actually a shocking realization when you first notice that your mind is constantly talking. You might even try to yell at it in a feeble attempt to shut it up. But then you realize that's the voice yelling at the voice:

> "Shut up! I want to go to sleep. Why do you have to talk all the time?"

The Voice Inside Your Head

Obviously, you can't shut it up that way. The best way to free yourself from this incessant chatter is to step back and view it objectively. Just view the voice as a vocalizing mechanism that is capable of making it appear like someone is in there talking to you. Don't think about it; just notice it. No matter what the voice is saying, it's all the same. It doesn't matter if it's saying nice things or mean things, worldly things or spiritual things. It doesn't matter because it's still just a voice talking inside your head. In fact, the only way to get your distance from this voice is to stop differentiating what it's saying. Stop feeling that one thing it says is you and the other thing it says is not you. If you're hearing it talk, it's obviously not you. You are the one who hears the voice. You are the one who notices that it's talking.

You do hear it when it talks, don't you? Make it say "hello" right now. Say it over and over a few times. Now shout it inside! Can you hear yourself saying "hello" inside? Of course you can. There is a voice talking, and there is you who notices the voice talking. The problem is that it's easy to notice the voice saying "hello," but it's difficult to see that no matter what the voice says, it is still just a voice talking and you listening. There is absolutely nothing that voice can say that is more you than anything else it says. Suppose you were looking at three objects—a flowerpot, a photograph, and a book—and

11

were then asked, "Which of these objects is you?" You'd say, "None of them! I'm the one who's looking at what you're putting in front of me. It doesn't matter what you put in front of me, it's always going to be me looking at it." You see, it's an act of a subject perceiving various objects. This is also true of hearing the voice inside. It doesn't make any difference what it's saying, you are the one who is aware of it. As long as you think that one thing it's saying is you, but the other thing it's saying is not you, you've lost your objectivity. You may want to think of yourself as the part that says the nice things, but that's still the voice talking. You may like what it says, but it's not you.

There is nothing more important to true growth than realizing that you are not the voice of the mind— you are the one who hears it. If you don't understand this, you will try to figure out which of the many things the voice says is really you. People go through so many changes in the name of "trying to find myself." They want to discover which of these voices, which of these aspects of their personality, is who they really are. The answer is simple: none of them.

If you watch it objectively, you will come to see that much of what the voice says is meaningless. Most of the talking is just a waste of time and energy. The truth is that most of life will unfold in accordance with forces far outside your control, regardless of what your mind says about it. It's like sitting down at night and deciding whether you want the sun to come up in the morning. The bottom line is, the sun will come up and the sun will go down. Billions of things are going on in this world. You can think about it all you want, but life is still going to keep on happening.

In fact, your thoughts have far less impact on this world than you would like to think. If you're willing to be objective and watch all your thoughts, you will see that the vast majority of them have no relevance. They have no effect on anything or anybody, except you. They are simply making you feel better or worse about what is going on now, what has gone on in the past, or what might go on in the future. If you spend your time hoping that it doesn't rain tomorrow, you are wasting your time. Your thoughts don't change the rain. You will someday come to see that there is no use for that incessant internal chatter, and there is no reason to constantly attempt to figure everything out. Eventually you will see that the real cause of problems is not life itself. It's the commotion the mind makes about life that really causes problems.

Now this raises a serious question: If so much of what the voice says is meaningless and unnecessary, then why does it even exist? The secret to answering this question lies in understanding why it says what it says when it says it. For example, in some cases the mental voice talks for the same reason that a teakettle whistles. That is, there's a buildup of energy inside that needs to be released. If you watch objectively, you will see that when there's a buildup of nervous, fearful, or desire-based energies inside, the voice becomes extremely active. This is easy to see when you are angry with someone and you feel like telling them off. Just watch how many times the inner voice tells them off before you even see them. When energy builds up inside, you want to do something about it. That voice talks because you're not okay inside, and talking releases energy.

You will notice, however, that even when you're not particularly bothered by something, it still talks. When you're walking down the street it says things like,

> "Look at that dog! It's a Labrador! Hey, there's another dog in that car. He looks a lot like my first dog, Shadow. Whoa, there's an old Oldsmobile. It's got Alaska plates. You don't see many of those down here!"

It is actually narrating the world for you. But why do you need this? You already see what's happening outside; how does it help to repeat it to yourself through the mental voice? You should examine this very closely. With a simple glance, you instantly take in the tremendous detail of whatever you're looking at. If you see a tree, you effortlessly see the branches, the leaves, and the flowering buds. Why then do you have to verbalize what you have already seen?

> "Look at that dogwood. The green leaves are
> so beautiful against the white flowers. Look
> how many flowers there are. Wow, it's so full!"

What you'll see, if you study this carefully, is that the narration makes you feel more comfortable with the world around you. Like backseat driving, it makes you feel as though things are more in your control. You actually feel like you have some relationship with them. A tree is no longer just a tree in the world that has nothing to do with you; it is a tree that you saw, labeled, and judged. By verbalizing it mentally, you brought that initial direct experience of the world into the realm of your thoughts. There it becomes integrated with your other thoughts, such as those making up your value system and historical experiences.

Take a moment to examine the difference between your experience of the outside world and your interactions with the mental world. When you're just thinking, you're free to create whatever thoughts you want in your mind, and these thoughts are expressed through the voice. You are very accustomed to settling into the playground of the mind and creating and manipulating thoughts. This inner world is an alternate environment that is under your control. The outside world, however, marches to its own laws. When the voice narrates the outside world to you, those thoughts are now side by side, in parity, with all your other thoughts. All these thoughts intermix and actually influence your experience of the world around you. What you end up experiencing is really a personal presentation of the world according to you, rather than the stark, unfiltered experience of what is really out there. This mental manipulation of the outer experience allows you to buffer reality as it comes in. For example, there are myriad things that you see at any given moment, yet you only narrate a few of them. The ones you discuss in your mind are the ones that matter to you. With this subtle form of preprocessing, you manage to control the experience of reality so that it all fits together inside your mind. Your consciousness is actually experiencing your mental model of reality, not reality itself.

You have to watch this very carefully because you do it all the time. You're walking outside in the winter, you start to shiver, and the voice says, "It's cold!" Now how did that help you? You already knew it was cold. You're the one who's experiencing the cold. Why is it telling you this? You re-create the world within your mind because you can control your mind whereas you can't control the world. That is why you mentally talk about it. If you can't get the world the way you like it, you internally verbalize it, judge it, complain about it, and then decide what to do about it. This makes you feel more empowered. When your body experiences cold, there may be nothing you can do to affect the temperature. But when your mind verbalizes, "It's cold!" you can say, "We're almost home, just a few more minutes." Now you feel better. In the thought world there's always something you can do to control the experience.

Basically, you re-create the outside world inside yourself, and then you live in your mind. What if you decided not to do this? If you decide not to narrate and, instead, just consciously observe the world, you will feel more open and exposed. This is because you really don't know what will happen next, and your mind is accustomed to helping you. It does this by processing your current experiences in a way that makes them fit with your views of the past and visions of the future. All of this helps to create a semblance of control. If your mind doesn't do this, you simply become too uncomfortable. Reality is just too real for most of us, so we temper it with the mind.

You will come to see that the mind talks all the time because you gave it a job to do. You use it as a protection mechanism, a form of defense. Ultimately, it makes you feel more secure. As long as that's what you want, you will be forced to constantly use your mind to buffer yourself from life, instead of living it. This world is unfolding and really has very little to do with you or your thoughts. It was here long before you came, and it will be here long after you leave. In the name of attempting to hold the world together, you're really just trying to hold yourself together.

True personal growth is about transcending the part of you that is not okay and needs protection. This is done by constantly remembering that you are the one inside that notices the voice talking. That is the way out. The one inside who is aware that you are always talking to yourself about yourself is always silent. It is a doorway to the depths of your being. To be aware that you are watching the voice talk is to stand on the threshold of a fantastic inner journey. If used properly, the same mental voice that has been a source of worry, distraction, and general neurosis can become the launching ground for true spiritual awakening. Come to know the one who watches the voice, and you will come to know one of the great mysteries of creation.

CHAPTER 2

your inner
roommate

Your inner growth is completely dependent upon the realization that the only way to find peace and contentment is to stop thinking about yourself. You're ready to grow when you finally realize that the "I" who is always talking inside will never be content. It always has a problem with something. Honestly, when was the last time you really had nothing bothering you? Before you had your current problem, there was a different problem. And if you're wise, you will realize that after this one's gone, there will be another one.

The bottom line is, you'll never be free of problems until you are free from the part within that has so many problems. When a problem is disturbing you, don't ask, "What should I do about it?" Ask, "What part of me is being disturbed by this?" If you ask, "What should I do about it?" you've already fallen into believing that there really is a problem outside that must be dealt with. If you want to achieve peace in the face of your problems, you must understand why you perceive a particular situation as a problem. If you're feeling jealousy, instead of trying to see how you can protect yourself, just ask, "What part of me is jealous?" That will cause you to look inside and see that there's a part of you that's having a problem with jealousy.

Your Inner Roommate

Once you clearly see the disturbed part, then ask, "Who is it that sees this? Who notices this inner disturbance?" Asking this is the solution to your every problem. The very fact that you can see the disturbance means that you are not it. The process of seeing something requires a subject-object relationship. The subject is called "The Witness" because it is the one who sees what's happening. The object is what you are seeing, in this case the inner disturbance. This act of maintaining objective awareness of the inner problem is always better than losing yourself in the outer situation. This is the essential difference between a spiritually minded person and a worldly person. Worldly doesn't mean that you have money or stature. Worldly means that you think the solution to your inner problems is in the world outside. You think that if you change things outside, you'll be okay. But nobody has ever truly become okay by changing things outside. There's always the next problem. The only real solution is to take the seat of witness consciousness and completely change your frame of reference.

To attain true inner freedom, you must be able to objectively watch your problems instead of being lost in them. No solution can possibly exist while you're lost in the energy of a problem. Everyone knows you can't deal well with a situation if you're getting anxious, scared, or angry about it. The first problem you have to deal with is your own reaction. You will not be able to solve anything outside until you own how the situation affects you inside. Problems are generally not what they appear to be. When you get clear enough, you will realize that the real problem is that there is something inside of you that can have a problem with almost anything. The first step is to deal with that part of you. This involves a change from "outer solution consciousness" to "inner solution consciousness." You have to break the habit of thinking that the solution to your problems is to rearrange things outside. The only permanent solution to your problems is to go inside and let go of the part of you that seems to have so many problems with reality. Once you do that, you'll be clear enough to deal with what's left.

There really is a way to let go of the part of you that sees everything as a problem. It may seem impossible, but it's not. There is a part of your being that can actually abstract from your own melodrama. You can watch yourself be jealous or angry. You don't have to think about it or analyze it; you can just be aware of it. Who is it that sees all this? Who notices the changes going on inside? When you tell a friend, "Every time I talk to Tom, it gets me so upset," how do you know it gets you upset? You know that it gets you upset because you're in there and you see what's going on in there. There's a separation between you and the anger or the jealousy. You are the one who's in there noticing these things. Once you take that seat of consciousness, you can get rid of these personal disturbances. You start by watching. Just be aware that you are aware of what is going on in there. It's easy. What you'll notice is that you're watching a human being's personality with all its strengths and weaknesses. It's as though there's somebody in there with you. You might actually say you have a "roommate."

If you would like to meet your roommate, just try to sit inside yourself for a while in complete solitude and silence. You have the right; it's your inner domain. But instead of finding silence, you're going to listen to incessant chatter:

> "Why am I doing this? I have more impor-
> tant things to do. This is a waste of time.
> There's nobody in here but me. What's this
> all about?"

Right on cue, there's your roommate. You may have a clear intention to be quiet inside, but your roommate won't cooperate. And it's not just when you try to be quiet. It has something to say about everything you look at: "I like it. I don't like it. This is good. That's bad." It just talks and talks. You don't generally notice because you don't step back from it. You're so close that you don't realize that you're actually hypnotized into listening to it.

Basically, you're not alone in there. There are two distinct aspects of your inner being. The first is you, the awareness, the witness, the center of your willful intentions; and the other is that which you watch. The problem is, the part that you watch never shuts up. If you could get rid of that part, even for a moment, the peace and serenity would be the nicest vacation you've ever had.

Imagine what it would be like if you didn't have to bring this thing with you everywhere you go. Real spiritual growth is about getting out of this predicament. But first you have to realize that you've been locked in there with a maniac. In any situation or circumstance, your roommate could suddenly decide, "I don't want to be here. I don't want to do this. I don't want to talk to this person." You would immediately feel tense and uncomfortable. Your roommate can ruin anything you're doing without a moment's notice. It could ruin your wedding day, or even your wedding night! That part of you can ruin anything and everything, and it generally does.

You buy a brand-new car and it's beautiful. But every time you drive it, your inner roommate finds something wrong with it. The mental voice keeps pointing out every little squeak, every little vibration, until eventually you don't even like the car anymore. Once you see what this can do to your life, you are ready for spiritual growth. You're ready for real transformation when you finally say, "Look at this thing. It's ruining my life. I'm trying to live a peaceful, meaningful existence, but I feel like I'm sitting on top of a volcano. At any moment this thing can decide to freak, close down, and fight with what's happening. One day it likes someone, and the next day it decides to pick on everything they do. My life is a mess just because this thing that lives in here with me has to make a melodrama out of everything." Once you've seen this, and learn to no longer identify with your roommate, you're ready to free yourself.

If you haven't reached this awareness yet, just start to watch. Spend a day watching every single thing your roommate does. Start in the morning and see if you can notice what it's saying in every situation. Every time you meet somebody, every time the phone rings, just try to watch. A good time to watch it talk is while you're taking a shower. Just watch what that voice has to say. You will see that it never lets you just take a peaceful shower. Your shower is for washing the body, not for watching the mind talk nonstop. See if you can stay conscious enough throughout the entire experience to be aware of what's going on. You'll be shocked by what you see. It just jumps from one subject to the next. The incessant chatter seems so neurotic that you won't believe that it's always that way. But it is.

You have to watch this if you want to be free of it. You don't have to do anything about it, but you have to get wise to the predicament you're in. You have to realize that somehow you've ended up with a mess for an inner roommate. If you want it to be peaceful in there, you're going to have to fix this situation.

The way to catch on to what your inner roommate is really like is to personify it externally. Make believe that your roommate, the psyche, has a body of its own. You do this by taking the entire personality that you hear talking to you inside and imagine it as a person talking to you on the outside. Just imagine that another person is now saying everything that your inner voice would say. Now spend a day with that person.

You've just sat down to watch your favorite TV show. The problem is, you have this person with you. Now you'll get to hear the same incessant monologue that used to be inside, except that it's sitting next to you on the couch talking to itself:

> "Did you turn off the light downstairs? You better go check. Not now, I'll do it later. I want to finish watching the show. No, do it now. That's why the electric bill is so high."

You sit in silent awe, watching all of this. Then, a few seconds later, your couch-mate is engaged in another dispute:

> "Hey, I want to get something to eat! I'm craving some pizza. No, you can't have pizza now; it's too far to drive. But I'm hungry. When will I get to eat?"

To your amazement, these neurotic bursts of conflicting dialogue just keep going on and on. And as if that's not enough, instead of simply watching TV, this person starts verbally reacting to whatever comes on the screen. At one point, after a redhead appears on the show, your couch-mate starts mumbling about an ex-spouse and a painful divorce. Then the yelling starts—just as though the ex-spouse were in the room with you! Then it stops, just as suddenly as it started. At this point, you find yourself hugging the far corner of the couch in a desperate attempt to get as far away from this disturbed person as you possibly can.

Will you dare to do this experiment? Don't try to make the person stop talking. Just try to get to know what you live with inside by externalizing the voice. Give it a body and put it out there in the world just like everybody else. Let it be a person who says on the outside exactly what the voice of your mind says inside. Now make that person your best friend. After all, how many friends do you spend all of your time with and pay absolute attention to every word they say?

How would you feel if someone outside really started talking to you the way your inner voice does? How would you relate to a person who opened their mouth to say everything your mental voice says? After a very short period of time, you would tell them to leave and never come back. But when your inner friend continuously speaks up, you don't ever tell it to leave. No matter how much trouble it causes, you listen. There's almost nothing that voice can say that you don't pay full attention to. It pulls you right out of whatever you're doing, no matter how enjoyable, and suddenly you're paying attention to whatever it has to say. Imagine that you're in a serious relationship and are about to get married. You're driving to the wedding and it says,

> "Maybe this is not the right person. I'm really getting nervous about this. What should I do?"

If someone outside of you said that, you'd ignore them. But you feel you owe the voice an answer. You have to convince your nervous mind that this is the right person, or it won't let you walk down the aisle. That's how much respect you have for this neurotic thing inside of you. You know that if you don't listen to it, it will bother you every day of your life:

> "I told you not to get married. I said I wasn't sure!"

The bottom line is undeniable: If somehow that voice managed to manifest in a body outside of you, and you had to take it with you everywhere you went, you wouldn't last a day. If somebody were to ask you what your new friend is like, you'd say, "This is one seriously disturbed person. Just look up neurosis in the dictionary and you'll get the picture."

That being the case, once you've spent a day with your friend, what is the probability you'd go to them for advice? After seeing how often this person changed their mind, how conflicted they were on so many subjects, and how emotionally overreactive they tended to be, would you ever ask them for relationship or financial advice? As amazing as it seems, you do just that every moment of your life. Having taken its rightful place back inside of you, it is still the same "person" who tells you what to do about every aspect of your life. Have you ever bothered to check its credentials? How many times has that voice been totally wrong?

> "She doesn't care for you anymore. That's why she hasn't called. She's going to break up with you tonight. I can feel it coming; I just know it. You shouldn't even answer the phone if she calls."

After thirty minutes of this, the phone rings and it's your girlfriend. She's late because it's your one-year anniversary and she was preparing for a surprise dinner. It was definitely a surprise to you, since you completely forgot the anniversary. She says she's on her way over to pick you up. Well, you're very excited and your inner voice is chatting about how great she is. But haven't you forgotten something? Haven't you forgotten about the bad advice the inner voice gave you that caused you to suffer for the last half hour?

What if you had hired a relationship advisor who had given you that terrible advice? They had completely misread the entire situation. Had you listened to the advisor, you never would have picked up the phone. Wouldn't you fire them on the spot? How could you ever trust their advice again after seeing how wrong they were? Well, are you going to fire your inner roommate?

Your Inner Roommate

After all, its advice and analysis of the situation were totally wrong. No, you never hold it responsible for the trouble it causes. In fact, the next time it gives advice, you're all ears. Is that rational? How many times has that voice been wrong about what was going on or what will be going on? Maybe it's worth noticing whom you're going to for advice.

When you've sincerely tried these practices of self-observation and awareness, you'll see that you're in trouble. You'll realize that you've only had one problem your entire life, and you're looking at it. It's pretty much the cause of every problem you've ever had. Now the question becomes, how do you get rid of this inner troublemaker? The first thing you'll realize is that there's no hope of getting rid of it until you really want to. Until you've watched your roommate long enough to truly understand the predicament you're in, you really have no basis for practices that help you deal with the mind. Once you've made the decision to free yourself from the mental melodrama, you are ready for teachings and techniques. You will now have a real use for them.

You will be relieved to know that you are not the first person to have this problem. There are those who have gone before you who found themselves in the same situation. Many of them looked for guidance from those who had mastered this field of knowledge. They were given teachings and techniques, such as yoga, which were created to help in this process. Yoga is not really about getting your body healthy, although it does that too. Yoga is about the knowledge that will help you out of your predicament, the knowledge that can free you. Once you've made this freedom the meaning of your life, there are spiritual practices that can help you. These practices are what you do with your time in order to free yourself from yourself. You will eventually catch on that you have to distance yourself from your psyche. You do this by setting the direction of your life when you're clear and not letting the wavering mind deter you. Your will is stronger than the habit of listening to that voice. There is nothing you can't do. Your will is supreme over all of this.

If you want to free yourself, you must first become conscious enough to understand your predicament. Then you must commit yourself to the inner work of freedom. You do this as though your life depended on it, because it does. As it is right now, your life is not your own; it belongs to your inner roommate, the psyche. You have to take it back. Stand firm in the seat of the witness and release the hold that the habitual mind has on you. This is your life—reclaim it.

CHAPTER 3

who are you?

The Untethered Soul

Ramana Maharshi (1879-1950), a great teacher in the yogic tradition, used to say that to attain inner freedom one must continuously and sincerely ask the question "Who am I?" He taught that this was more important than reading books, learning mantras, or going to holy places. Just ask, "Who am I? Who sees when I see? Who hears when I hear? Who knows that I am aware? Who am I?"

Let's explore this question by playing a game. Make believe that you and I are having a conversation. Typically, in Western cultures, when someone comes up to you and asks, "Excuse me, who are you?" you don't admonish them for asking such a deep question. You tell them your name, for example, Sally Smith. But I'm going to challenge this response by taking out a piece of paper and writing the letters S-a-l-l-y S-m-i-t-h, and then showing it to you. Is that who you are—a collection of letters? Is that who sees when you see? Obviously not, so you say,

> "Okay, you're right, I'm sorry. I'm not Sally Smith. That's just a name people call me. It's a label. Really, I'm Frank Smith's wife."

No way, that's not even politically correct nowadays. How could you be Frank Smith's wife? Are you saying you didn't exist before you met Frank, and you would cease to exist if he died or you got remarried? Frank Smith's wife can't be who you are. Again, that's just another label, the result of another situation or event you participated in. But then, who are you? This time you respond,

> "Okay, now you have my attention. My label is Sally Smith. I was born in 1965 in New York. I lived in Queens with my parents, Harry and Mary Jones, until I was five years old. Then we moved to New Jersey and I went to Newark Elementary School. I got all A's in school, and in the fifth grade I played Dorothy in the Wizard of Oz. I started dating in the ninth grade, and my first boyfriend was Joe. I went to Rutgers College where I met and married Frank Smith. That is who I am."

Wait a minute, that's a fascinating story, but I didn't ask you what has happened to you since you were born. I asked you, "Who are you?" You've just described all these experiences, but who had these experiences? Wouldn't you still be in there, aware of your existence, even if you had gone to a different college?

So you contemplate this, and you realize that never in your life have you asked yourself that question and really meant it. Who am I? That is what Ramana Maharshi was asking. So you ponder this more seriously and you say,

> "Okay, I am the body that is occupying this space. I am five foot six and I weigh 135 pounds, and here I am."

When you were Dorothy in the fifth grade play you weren't five foot six, you were four foot six. So which are you? Are you the four foot six person or are you the five foot six person? Weren't you in there when you were Dorothy? You told me you were. Aren't you the one who had the experience of being Dorothy in the fifth grade play and is now having the experience of trying to answer my questions? Isn't this the same you?

Perhaps we need to step back for a moment to ask some exploratory questions before returning to the core question. When you were ten years old, didn't you look in the mirror and see a ten-year-old body? Wasn't that the same you that now sees an adult body? What you looked at has changed; but what about you, the one who is looking? Isn't there a continuity of being? Wasn't it the same being that looked in the mirror throughout the years? You have to contemplate this very carefully. Here's another question: When you go to sleep every night, do you dream? Who dreams? What does it mean to dream? You answer, "Well, it's like a motion picture plays in my mind and I watch it." Who watches it? "I do!" The same you who looks in the mirror? Does the same you who is reading these words also look in the mirror and watch the dreams? When you awake, you know you saw the dream. There is a continuity of conscious awareness of being. Ramana Maharshi was just asking some very simple questions: Who sees when you see? Who hears when you hear? Who watches the dreams? Who looks at the image in the mirror? Who is it that is having all these experiences? If you try to just give honest, intuitive answers, you are simply going to say, "Me. It's me. I'm in here experiencing all of this." That's about the best answer you'll have.

It's actually pretty easy to see that you're not the objects you look at. It's a classic case of subject-object. It's you, the subject, that is looking at the objects. So we don't have to go through every object in the universe and say that object is not you. We can very easily generalize by saying that if you are the one who is looking at something, then that something is not you. So right away, in one fell swoop, you know what you're not: you're not the outside world. You're the one who is inside looking out at that world.

That was easy. Now at least we've eliminated the countless things outside. But who are you? And where are you if you're not outside with all the other things? You just have to pay attention and realize that you would still be in there experiencing feelings even if all the outside objects disappeared. Imagine how much fear you would feel. You might also feel frustration, and even anger. But who would be feeling these things? Again you say "Me!" And that's the right answer. The same "me" experiences both the outside world and the inside emotions.

To take a clear look at this, imagine that you're watching a dog play outdoors. Suddenly you hear a noise right behind you—a hiss, like a rattlesnake! Would you still be looking at the dog with the same intensity of focus? Of course not. You'd be feeling tremendous fear inside. Though the dog would still be playing in front of you, you'd be completely preoccupied with the experience of fear. All of your attention can very quickly become absorbed in your emotions. But who feels the fear? Isn't it the same you who was watching the dog? Who feels love when you feel love? Can't you feel so much love that it's hard to keep your eyes open? You can become so absorbed in beautiful inner feelings, or frightening inner fears, that it's hard to focus on outer objects.

Who Are You?

In essence, inside and outside objects compete for your attention. You are in there having both inner and outer experiences—but who are you?

To explore this more deeply, answer another question: Don't you have times when you're not having emotional experiences and, instead, you just feel quiet inside? You're still in there, but you're just aware of peaceful quiet. Eventually, you will begin to realize that the outside world and the flow of inner emotions come and go. But you, the one who experiences these things, remain consciously aware of whatever passes before you.

But where are you? Maybe we can find you in your thoughts. René Descartes, a great philosopher, once said, "I think, therefore I am." But is that really what's going on? The dictionary defines the verb "to think" as "to form thoughts, to use the mind to consider ideas and make judgments" (Microsoft Encarta 2007). The question is, who is using the mind to form thoughts and then manipulate them into ideas and judgments? Does this experiencer of thoughts exist even when thoughts are not present? Fortunately, you don't have to think about it. You are very aware of your presence of being, your sense of existence, without the help of thoughts. When you go into deep meditation, for example, the thoughts stop. You know that they've stopped. You don't "think" it, you are simply aware of "no thoughts." You come back and say, "Wow, I went into this deep meditation, and for the first time my thoughts completely stopped. I was in a place of complete peace, harmony, and quiet." If you are in there experiencing the peace that occurs when your thoughts stop, then obviously your existence is not dependent upon the act of thinking.

Thoughts can stop, and they can also get extremely noisy. Sometimes you have many more thoughts than other times. You may even tell someone, "My mind is driving me crazy. Ever since he said those things to me, I can't even sleep. My mind just won't shut up." Whose mind? Who is noticing these thoughts? Isn't it you? Don't you hear your thoughts inside? Aren't you aware of their existence? In fact, can't you get rid of them? If you start to have a thought you don't like, can't you try to make it go away? People struggle with thoughts all the time. Who is it that is aware of the thoughts, and who is it that struggles with them? Again, you have a subject-object relationship with your thoughts. You are the subject, and thoughts are just another object you can be aware of. You are not your thoughts. You are simply aware of your thoughts. Finally you say,

> "Fine, I'm not anything in the outside world and I'm not the emotions. These outer and inner objects come and go and I experience

them. Plus, I'm not the thoughts. They can be quiet or noisy, happy or sad. Thoughts are just something else I'm aware of. But who am I?"

It starts to become a serious question: "Who am I? Who is having all these physical, emotional, and mental experiences?" So you contemplate this question a little deeper. This is done by letting go of the experiences and noticing who is left. You will begin to notice who is experiencing the experience. Eventually, you will get to a point within yourself where you realize that you, the experiencer, have a certain quality. And that quality is awareness, consciousness, an intuitive sense of existence. You know that you're in there. You don't have to think about it; you just know. You can think about it if you want to, but you will know that you're thinking about it. You exist regardless, thoughts or no thoughts.

To make this more experiential, let's try a consciousness experiment. Notice that with a single glance at a room, or out a window, you instantaneously see the full detail of everything that's in front of you. You are effortlessly aware of all the objects that are within the scope of your vision, both near and far away. Without moving your head or eyes, you perceive all the intricate detail of what you immediately see. Look at all the colors, the variations of light, the grain of wood furniture, the architecture of buildings, and the variations of bark and leaves on trees. Notice that you take all this in at once, without having to think about it. No thoughts are necessary; you just see it. Now try to use thoughts to isolate, label, and describe all the intricate detail of what you see. How long would it take your mental voice to describe all that detail to you, versus the instantaneous snapshot of consciousness just seeing? When you just look without creating thoughts, your consciousness is effortlessly aware of, and fully comprehends, all that it sees.

Consciousness is the highest word you will ever utter. There is nothing higher or deeper than consciousness. Consciousness is pure awareness. But what is awareness? Let's try another experiment. Let's say you are in a room looking at a group of people and a piano. Now make believe the piano ceases to exist in your world. Would you have a major problem with that? You say, "No, I don't think so. I'm not attached to pianos." Okay then, make believe the people in the room cease to exist. Are you still okay? Can you handle it? You say, "Sure, I like being alone." Now make believe your awareness doesn't exist. Just turn it off. How are you doing now?

What would it be like if your awareness didn't exist? It's actually pretty simple—you wouldn't be there. There would be no sense of "me." There wouldn't be anyone in there to say, "Wow, I used to be in here but now I'm not." There would no longer be an awareness of being. And without awareness of being, or consciousness, there is nothing. Are there objects? Who knows? If no one is aware of the objects, their existence or nonexistence becomes completely irrelevant. It doesn't matter how many things are in front of you; if you turn off the consciousness, there is nothing. If you are conscious, however, there can be nothing in front of you but you are fully aware that there is nothing. It's really not that complicated, and it's very enlightening.

So now if I ask you, "Who are you?" you answer,

> "I am the one who sees. From back in here somewhere, I look out, and I am aware of the events, thoughts, and emotions that pass before me."

If you go very deep, that is where you live. You live in the seat of consciousness. A true spiritual being lives there, without effort and without intent. Just as you effortlessly look outside and see all that you see, you will eventually sit far enough back inside to see all your thoughts and emotions, as well as outer form. All of these objects are in front of you. The thoughts are closer in, the emotions are a little further away, and form is way out there. Behind it all, there you are. You go so deep that you realize that's where you've always been. At each stage of your life you have seen different thoughts, emotions, and objects pass before you. But you have always been the conscious receiver of all that was.

Now you are in your center of consciousness. You are behind everything, just watching. That is your true home. Take everything else away and you're still there, aware that everything is gone. But take the center of awareness away, and there is nothing. That center is the seat of Self. From that seat, you are aware that there are thoughts, emotions, and a world coming in through your senses. But now you are aware that you're aware. That is the seat of the Buddhist Self[1], the Hindu Atman[2], and the Judeo-Christian Soul. The great mystery begins once you take that seat deep within.

---

1   As explicated by the Buddha in the Mahayana Mahaparinirvana
     Sutra (trans. Kosho Yamamoto 1973).

2   Atman: *Hinduism* - The innermost essence of each individual
     (Merriam-Webster 2003).

CHAPTER 4

the lucid self

There is a type of dream, called a lucid dream, in which you know that you're dreaming. If you fly in the dream you know that you're flying. You think, "Hey, look! I'm dreaming that I'm flying. I'm going to fly over there." You are actually conscious enough to know that you are flying in the dream and that you are dreaming the dream. That's very different from regular dreams, in which you are fully immersed in the dream. This distinction is exactly the difference between being aware that you are aware in your daily life, and not being aware that you are aware. When you are an aware being, you no longer become completely immersed in the events around you. Instead, you remain inwardly aware that you are the one who is experiencing both the events and the corresponding thoughts and emotions. When a thought is created in this state of awareness, instead of getting lost in it, you remain aware that you are the one who is thinking the thought. You are lucid.

This raises some very interesting questions. If you are the indwelling being who is experiencing all this, then why do these different levels of perception exist? When you are seated in the awareness of Self, you are lucid. Where are you when you are not seated deeply enough inside the Self to be the conscious experiencer of all you are experiencing?

The Lucid Self

To begin with, consciousness has the ability to do what is called "focus." It is part of the nature of consciousness. The essence of consciousness is awareness, and awareness has the ability to become more aware of one thing and less aware of something else. In other words, it has the ability to focus itself on certain objects. The teacher says, "Concentrate on what I'm saying." What does that mean? It means focus your consciousness on one place. Teachers figure you know how to do that. Who taught you how to do that? What class in high school taught you how to take your consciousness and move it somewhere in order to focus on something? Nobody taught you this. It was intuitive and natural. You've always known how to do it.

So we do know that consciousness exists; we just don't normally talk about it. You probably went through grade school, high school, and college without anyone discussing the nature of consciousness. Fortunately, the nature of consciousness has been studied very closely in deep teachings such as yoga. In fact, the ancient teachings of yoga are all about consciousness.

The best way to learn about consciousness is through your own direct experience. For example, you know very well that your consciousness can be aware of a wide field of objects, or it can be so focused on one object that you are unaware of anything else. This is what happens when you get lost in thought. You can be reading, and then suddenly you're not reading anymore. It happens all the time. You just start thinking about something else. Outside objects or mental thoughts can catch your attention at any time. But it's still the same awareness, whether it is focused on the outside or on your thoughts.

The key is that consciousness has the ability to concentrate on different things. The subject, consciousness, has the ability to selectively focus awareness on specific objects. If you step back, you will clearly see that objects are constantly passing before you at all three levels: mental, emotional, and physical. When you're not centered, your consciousness invariably gets attracted toward one or more of those objects and focuses on them. If it concentrates enough, your sense of awareness loses itself in the object. It is no longer aware that it is aware of the object; it just becomes object-conscious. Have you ever noticed that when you're deeply absorbed in watching TV, you have no awareness of where you're sitting or what else is going on in the room?

The TV analogy is perfect for examining how our center of consciousness shifts from awareness of Self to being lost in the objects we're focused upon. The difference is that instead of sitting in your living room getting absorbed in the TV, you're sitting in your center of consciousness getting absorbed in the screens of mind, emotions, and outside images. When you concentrate on the world of the physical senses, it draws you in. Then your emotional and mental reactions draw you in further. At that point, you are no longer sitting in the centered Self; you are absorbed in the inner show you're watching.

Let's look at your inner show. You have an underlying pattern of thoughts that goes on around you all the time. This pattern of thoughts stays pretty much the same. You are as familiar and comfortable with your normal thought patterns as you are with the living space of your home. You also have emotions that are your norm: a certain amount of fear, a certain amount of love, and a certain amount of insecurity. You know that if certain things happen, one or more of these emotions will flare up and dominate your awareness. Then, eventually, they will settle back down to the norm. You know this so well that you are very busy inside making sure nothing happens to create these disturbances. In fact, you are so preoccupied with controlling your world of thoughts, emotions, and physical sensations that you don't even know you're in there. That is the normal state for most people.

When you are in this lost state, you get so totally absorbed in the objects of thoughts, feelings, and the senses, that you forget the subject. Right now, you are sitting inside the center of consciousness watching your personal TV show. But there are so many interesting objects distracting your consciousness that you can't help but get drawn into them. It's overwhelming. It's three-dimensional. It's all around you. All of your senses draw you in—sight, sound, taste, smell, and touch—as well as your feelings and your thoughts. But you are really sitting quietly inside looking out at all these objects. Just as the sun does not leave its position in the sky to illuminate objects with its radiating light, so consciousness does not leave its center to project awareness onto the objects of form, thoughts, and emotions. If you ever want to re-center, just start saying "hello" inside, over and over. Then notice that you are aware of that thought. Don't think about being aware of it; that's just another thought. Simply relax and be aware that you can hear "hello" being echoed in your mind. That is your seat of centered consciousness.

Now let's move from the small screen to the big one. Let's study consciousness using the example of a movie. When you go to a movie, you let yourself get drawn in. It's part of the experience of watching the movie. With a movie you use two senses: seeing and hearing. And it's very important that these senses synchronize. You wouldn't get as involved in the film if they didn't. Imagine if you were watching a James Bond movie and the soundtrack didn't synchronize with the scenes. Instead of getting drawn into the magical world of the movie, you would remain very aware that you were sitting in a theater and that something was wrong. But because soundtracks and scenes normally synchronize perfectly, movies capture your awareness and you forget that you're sitting in the theater. You forget your personal thoughts and emotions, and your consciousness gets pulled into the film. It's actually quite phenomenal to contemplate the difference between the experience of sitting next to strangers in a cold, dark theater versus being so absorbed in the movie that you are totally unaware of your surroundings. In fact, with an engaging film, you may go for the full two hours without any awareness of yourself. So the synchronization of sight and sound is very important if your consciousness is to become absorbed in the movie. And that's just two of your senses.

What will happen when your experience of a movie includes smell and taste? Imagine that you're experiencing a film in which someone is eating and you taste what they taste and smell what they smell. You would surely get caught in that one. The sensory input has doubled and therefore the number of objects drawing on your consciousness has also doubled. Sound, sight, taste, smell, and we haven't mentioned the big one yet—

would you even go to a theater that has touch? When they get all five senses working together, you don't stand a chance. If they all synchronize, you'll be completely absorbed into the experience. But then again, not necessarily. Imagine you're sitting in the theater, and even with this overwhelming sensory experience, you still become bored with the movie. It just isn't capturing your attention, so your thoughts start to wander. You begin thinking about what you'll do when you get home. You start thinking about something that happened to you in the past. After a while, you're so lost in your thoughts that you're hardly aware that you're watching a movie. This occurs despite the fact that your five senses are still sending you all these movie messages. This can only happen because your thoughts can still occur independently of the movie. They provide an alternative place for the consciousness to focus.

Now imagine that movies are made that not only engage the five senses, but also make your thoughts and emotions synchronize with what's happening on the screen. With this movie experience, you're hearing, seeing, tasting, and suddenly you begin feeling the character's emotions and thinking the character's thoughts. The character says, "I'm so nervous. Should I ask her to marry me?" and suddenly insecurity wells up inside of you. Now we have the full dimension of the experience: five physical senses, plus thoughts and emotions. Imagine going to that movie and getting plugged in. Careful, that would be the end of you as you know yourself. There would be no object of consciousness that is not synchronized with the experience. Any place your awareness falls would be part of the movie. Once the movie gets control of the thoughts, it's over. There is no "you" in there saying, "I don't like this movie. I want to leave." That would take an independent thought, but your thoughts have been taken over by the movie. Now you are completely lost. How will you ever get out?

As scary as it sounds, that is your predicament in life. Because all of the objects you're aware of are synchronized, you get sucked in and are no longer aware of your separateness from the objects. The thoughts and the emotions move in accordance with the sights and the sounds. It all comes in, and your consciousness gets totally absorbed in it. Unless you're fully seated in witness consciousness, you're not back there being aware that you're the one watching all this. That is what it means to be lost.

The lost soul is the consciousness that has dropped into the place where one human's thoughts, emotions, and sensory perceptions of sight, sound, taste, touch, and smell are all synchronized. All these messages come back to one spot. Then the consciousness, which is capable of being aware of anything, makes the mistake of focusing on that one spot too closely. When the consciousness gets sucked in, it no longer knows itself as itself. It knows itself as the objects it is experiencing. In other words, you perceive yourself as these objects. You think you are the sum of your learned experiences.

That is what you would think when you go to one of these advanced movies. At such a movie, you would first get to select which character you want to be. Let's say you decide, "I'll be James Bond." Okay, but once you push the button, that's it. The button had better be on a timer! You, as you currently know yourself, are no longer there. Since all of your thoughts are now James Bond's thoughts, your entire existing self-concept is gone. Remember, your self-concept is just a collection of thoughts about yourself. Likewise, your emotions are Bond's and you are watching the movie through his visual and auditory perspective. The only aspect of your being that remains the same is the consciousness that is aware of these objects. It is the same center of awareness that was aware of your old set of thoughts, emotions, and sensory input. Now someone turns off the movie. Immediately, Bond's thoughts and emotions are replaced with your old set of thoughts and emotions. You're back to thinking that you're a forty-year-old woman. All the thoughts match. All the emotions match. Everything looks like, smells like, tastes like, and feels like it did before. But that doesn't change the fact that it is all just something consciousness is experiencing. It is all just objects of consciousness, and you are the consciousness.

What differentiates a conscious, centered being from a person who is not so conscious is simply the focus of their awareness. It's not a difference in the consciousness itself. All consciousness is the same. Just as all light from the sun is the same, all awareness is the same. Consciousness is neither pure nor impure; it has no qualities. It's just there, aware that it's aware. The difference is that when your consciousness is not centered within, it becomes totally focused on the objects of consciousness. When you are a centered being, however, your consciousness is always aware of being conscious. Your awareness of being is independent of the inner and outer objects you happen to be aware of.

If you really want to understand this difference, you must begin by realizing that consciousness can focus on anything. That being the case, what if consciousness were to focus on itself? When that happens, instead of being aware of your thoughts, you're aware that you're aware of your thoughts. You have turned the light of consciousness back onto itself. You're always contemplating something, but this time you're contemplating the source of consciousness. This is true meditation. True meditation is beyond the act of simple, one-pointed concentration. For the deepest meditation, you must not only have the ability to focus your consciousness completely on one object, you must also have the ability to make awareness itself be that object. In the highest state, the focus of consciousness is turned back to the Self.

When you contemplate the nature of Self, you are meditating. That is why meditation is the highest state. It is the return to the root of your being, the simple awareness of being aware. Once you become conscious of the consciousness itself, you attain a totally different state. You are now aware of who you are. You have become an awakened being. It's really just the most natural thing in the world. Here I am. Here I always was. It's like you have been on the couch watching TV, but you were so totally immersed in the show that you forgot where you were. Someone shook you, and now you're back to the awareness that you're sitting on the couch watching TV. Nothing else changed. You simply stopped projecting your sense of self onto that particular object of consciousness. You woke up. That is spirituality. That is the nature of Self. That is who you are.

As you pull back into the consciousness, this world ceases to be a problem. It's just something you're watching. It keeps changing, but there is no sense of that being a problem. The more you are willing to just let the world be something you're aware of, the more it will let you be who you are—the awareness, the Self, the Atman, the Soul.

You realize that you're not who you thought you were. You're not even a human being. You just happen to be watching one. You will begin to have deep experiences within your own center of consciousness. These will be deep, intuitive experiences of the true nature of Self. You will find that you are tremendously expansive. When you start to explore consciousness instead of form, you realize that your consciousness only appears to be small and limited because you are focusing on small and limited objects. That's exactly what happens when you're focusing solely on the TV—there's nothing else in your world. If you pull back, however, you can see the whole room, including the TV. Likewise, instead of just focusing so intently on this one human being's thoughts, emotions, and sensory world, you can pull back and see everything. You can move from the finite to the infinite. Isn't this what they've been trying to tell us—Christ, Buddha, and the great saints and sages of all time and all religions?

One of these great saints, Ramana Maharshi, used to ask, "Who am I?" We see now that this is a very deep question. Ask it ceaselessly, constantly. Ask it and you will notice that you are the answer. There is no intellectual answer—you are the answer. Be the answer, and everything will change.

PART II

experiencing energy

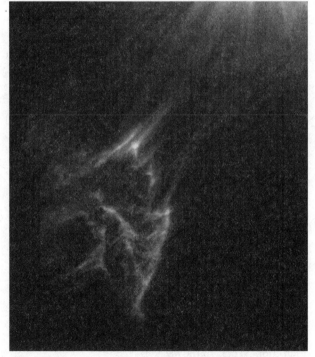

CHAPTER 5

infinite energy

The Untethered Soul

Consciousness is one of the great mysteries in life. Inner energy is another. It's actually a shame how little attention the Western world pays to the laws of inner energy. We study the energy outside, and give great value to energy resources, but we ignore the energy within. People go about their lives thinking, feeling, and acting, without the understanding of what makes these activities take place. The truth is, every movement of your body, every emotion you have, and every thought that passes through your mind is an expenditure of energy. Just as everything that happens outside in the physical world requires energy, everything that happens inside requires an expenditure of energy.

For example, if you concentrate on a thought and another thought interferes, you will have to assert an opposing force to fight the interfering thought. That requires energy, and it can wear you out. Likewise, if you have a thought that you're trying to hold in your mind but it keeps drifting off, you have to willfully concentrate to bring it back. When you do this, you are actually sending more energy to the thought in order to hold it in a given place. You also assert energy to deal with your emotions. If you have an emotion you don't like and it's interfering with what you're doing, you just push it aside. You do this almost instinctively so that the unwanted emotion doesn't come up and disturb you. Every one of these acts is an expenditure of energy.

Creating thoughts, holding onto thoughts, recalling thoughts, generating emotions, controlling emotions, and disciplining powerful inner drives, all require a tremendous expenditure of energy. Where does all this energy come from? Why is the energy there sometimes, and at other times you feel completely drained? Have you ever noticed that when you are mentally and emotionally drained, food doesn't help that much? Conversely, if you look at the times in your life when you were in love, or excited and inspired by something, you were so filled with energy that you didn't even want to eat. This energy we are discussing does not come from the calories your body burns from food. There is a source of energy you can draw upon from inside. It is distinct from the outer energy source.

The best way to examine this source of energy is to look at an example. Let's say that you're in your twenties and your girlfriend or boyfriend breaks up with you. You get so totally depressed that you start staying home alone. Soon, because you don't have the energy to clean up, everything ends up sprawled all over the floor. You can hardly get out of bed, so you just sleep all the time. You must be eating, because there are pizza boxes lying all around. But nothing seems to help. You just have no energy. Your friends invite you out, but you decline. You are simply too tired to do anything.

Most people have been there at some time in their lives. You feel that you have no way out, and it seems like you will stay there forever. Then suddenly, one day, the phone rings. It's your girlfriend. That's right, the one who dumped you three months ago. She's crying as she says, "Oh, my God! Do you remember me? I hope you'll still talk to me. I just feel so terrible. Leaving you was the worst mistake I ever made. I see now how important you are to me, and I can't live without you. The only real love I ever felt in my life was during the time we were together. Would you please forgive me? Could you ever forgive me? Can I come over and see you?"

Now how are you doing? Seriously, how long does it take you to get enough energy to jump out of bed, clean up the apartment, take a shower, and get some color back in your face? It's practically instantaneous. You're filled with energy the moment you hang up the phone. How does this happen? You were completely drained. For months and months, you had no energy. Then out of nowhere, in a matter of seconds, there is so much energy it blows you away.

You can't just ignore these enormous shifts in your energy level. Where exactly did all that energy come from? There was no sudden change in your eating or sleeping habits. Yet when your girlfriend comes by, you end up talking all night and going out to see the sunrise in the morning. You're not tired at all. You're together again and you're holding hands and these rushes of joy just won't stop overwhelming you. People see you and they remark that you look like a bundle of light. Where did all this energy come from?

What you'll see, if you watch carefully, is that you have a phenomenal amount of energy inside of you. It doesn't come from food and it doesn't come from sleep. This energy is always available to you. At any moment you can draw upon it. It just wells up and fills you from inside. When you're filled with this energy, you feel like you could take on the world. When it is flowing strongly, you can actually feel it coursing through you in waves. It gushes up spontaneously from deep inside and restores, replenishes, and recharges you.

The only reason you don't feel this energy all the time is because you block it. You block it by closing your heart, by closing your mind, and by pulling yourself into a restrictive space inside. This closes you off from all the energy. When you close your heart or close your mind, you hide in the darkness within you. There is no light. There is no energy. There is nothing flowing. The energy is still there but it can't get in.

That is what it means to be "blocked." That is why you have no energy when you're depressed. There are centers within that channel your energy flow. When you close them, there is no energy. When you open them, there is. Although various energy centers exist within you, the one you intuitively know the most about opening and closing is your heart. Let's say that you love somebody, and you feel very open in their presence. Because you trust them, your walls come down allowing you to feel lots of high energy. But if they do something you don't like, the next time you see them you don't feel so high. You don't feel as much love. Instead, you feel a tightness in your chest. This happens because you closed your heart. The heart is an energy center, and it can open or close. The yogis call energy centers *chakras*. When you close your heart center, energy can't flow in. When energy can't flow in, there's darkness. Depending upon how closed you are, you either feel tremendous disturbance or overwhelming lethargy. Often people fluctuate between these two states. If you then find out that your loved one didn't do anything wrong, or if they apologize to your satisfaction, your heart opens again. With this opening you get filled with energy, and the love starts flowing again.

How many times have you experienced these dynamics in your life? You have a wellspring of beautiful energy inside of you. When you are open you feel it; when you are closed you don't. This flow of energy comes from the depth of your being. It's been called by many names. In ancient Chinese medicine, it is called Chi. In yoga, it is called Shakti. In the West, it is called Spirit. Call it anything you want. All the great spiritual traditions talk about your spiritual energy; they just give it different names. That spiritual energy is what you're experiencing when love rushes up into your heart. That is what you're experiencing when you're enthused by something and all this high energy comes up inside of you.

You should know about this energy because it's yours. It's your birthright, and it's unlimited. You can call upon it any time you want. It has nothing to do with age. Some eighty-year-old people have the energy and enthusiasm of a child. They can work long hours for seven days a week. It's just energy. Energy doesn't get old, it doesn't get tired, and it doesn't need food. What it needs is openness and receptivity. This energy is equally available to everybody. The sun does not shine differently on different people. If you're good, it shines on you. If you did something bad, it shines on you. It's the same with the inner energy. The only difference is that with the inner energy, you have the ability to close up inside and block it. When you close, the energy stops flowing. When you open, all the energy rushes up inside of you.

True spiritual teachings are about this energy and how to open to it.

The only thing you have to know is that opening allows energy in, and closing blocks it out. Now you have to decide whether or not you want this energy. How high do you want to get? How much love do you want to feel? How much enthusiasm do you want to have for the things you do? If enjoying a full life means experiencing high energy, love, and enthusiasm all the time, then don't ever close.

There is a very simple method for staying open. You stay open by never closing. It's really that simple. All you have to do is decide whether you are willing to stay open, or whether you think it's worth closing. You can actually train yourself to forget how to close. Closing is a habit, and just like any other habit, it can be broken. For example, you could be the type of person who has an underlying fear of people and tends to close when you first meet them. You could actually be in the habit of experiencing an uptight, closing sensation whenever somebody walks up to you. You can train yourself to do the opposite. You can train yourself to open every time you see a person. It's just a question of whether you want to close or whether you want to open. It's ultimately under your control.

The problem is, we don't exercise that control. Under normal circumstances, our state of openness is left to psychological factors. Basically, we are programmed to open or close based upon our past experiences. Impressions from the past are still inside of us, and they get stimulated by different events. If they were negative impressions, we tend to close. If they were positive impressions, we tend to open. Let's say you smell a certain scent that reminds you of what it was like when you were young and somebody was cooking dinner. How you react to this scent depends upon the impressions left by your past experiences. Did you enjoy having dinner with the family? Was the food good? If so, then the smell of that scent warms you and opens you. If it wasn't so much fun eating together, or if you had to eat food you didn't like, then you tighten up and close. It really is that sensitive. A smell can make you open or close, and so can seeing a car of a certain color, or even the type of shoes a person is wearing. We are programmed based upon our past impressions such that all kinds of things can cause us to open and close. If you pay attention, you will see it happen regularly throughout each day.

But you should never leave something as important as your energy flow to chance. If you like energy, and you do, then don't ever close. The more you learn to stay open, the more the energy can flow into you. You practice opening by not closing. Any time you start to close, ask yourself whether you really want to cut off the energy flow. Because if you want, you can learn to stay open no matter what happens in this world. You just make a commitment to explore your capacity for receiving unlimited energy. You simply decide not to close. At first it feels unnatural since your innate tendency is to close as a means of protection. But closing your heart does not really protect you from anything; it just cuts you off from your source of energy. In the end, it only serves to lock you inside.

What you'll find is that the only thing you really want from life is to feel enthusiasm, joy, and love. If you can feel that all the time, then who cares what happens outside? If you can always feel up, if you can always feel excited about the experience of the moment, then it doesn't make any difference what the experience is. No matter what it is, it's beautiful when you feel that way inside. So you learn to stay open no matter what happens. If you do, you get for free what everybody else is struggling for: love, enthusiasm, excitement, and energy. You simply realize that defining what you need in order to stay open actually ends up limiting you. If you make lists of how the world must be for you to open, you have limited your openness to those conditions. Better to be open no matter what.

Infinite Energy

How you learn to stay open is up to you. The ultimate trick is to not close. If you don't close, you will have learned to stay open. Do not let anything that happens in life be important enough that you're willing to close your heart over it. When your heart starts to close, just say, "No. I'm not going to close. I'm going to relax. I'm going to let this situation take place and be there with it." Honor and respect the situation, and deal with it. By all means deal with it. Do the best you can. But deal with it with openness. Deal with it with excitement and enthusiasm. No matter what it is, just let it be the sport of the day. In time, you will find that you forget how to close. No matter what anyone does, no matter what situation takes place, you won't even feel the tendency to close. You will just embrace life with all your heart and soul. Once you've attained this very high state, your energy level will be phenomenal. You will have all the energy you need at all times. Just relax and open, and tremendous energy will rush up inside of you. You are only limited by your ability to stay open.

If you really want to stay open, pay attention when you feel love and enthusiasm. Then ask yourself why you can't feel this all the time. Why does it have to go away? The answer is obvious: it only goes away if you choose to close. By closing, you are actually making the choice not to feel openness and love. You throw love away all the time. You feel love until somebody says something you don't like, and then you give up the love. You feel enthused about your job until someone criticizes something, and then you want to quit. It's your choice. You can either close because you don't like what happened, or you can keep feeling love and enthusiasm by not closing. As long as you are defining what you like and what you don't like, you will open and close. You are actually defining your limits. You are allowing your mind to create triggers that open and close you. Let go of that. Dare to be different. Enjoy all of life.

The more you stay open, the more the energy flow can build. At some point, so much energy comes into you that it starts flowing out of you. You feel it as waves pouring off of you. You can actually feel it flowing off your hands, out your heart, and through other energy centers. All these energy centers open, and a tremendous amount of energy starts flowing out of you. What is more, the energy affects other people. People can pick up on your energy, and you're feeding them with this flow. If you are willing to open even more, it never stops. You become a source of light for all those around you.

Just keep opening and not closing. Wait until you see what happens to you. You can even affect the health of your body with your energy flow. When you start to feel the tendency of an illness coming on, you just relax and open. When you open, you bring more energy into the system, and it can heal. Energy can heal, and that's why love can heal. As you explore your inner energy, a whole world of discovery opens up to you.

The most important thing in life is your inner energy. If you're always tired and never enthused, then life is no fun. But if you're always inspired and filled with energy, then every minute of every day is an exciting experience. Learn to work with these things. Through meditation, through awareness and willful efforts, you can learn to keep your centers open. You do this by just relaxing and releasing. You do this by not buying into the concept that there is anything worth closing over. Remember, if you love life, nothing is worth closing over. Nothing, ever, is worth closing your heart over.

CHAPTER 6

the secrets of the spiritual heart

Very few people understand the heart. In truth, your heart is one of the masterpieces of creation. It is a phenomenal instrument. It has the potential to create vibrations and harmonies that are far beyond the beauty of pianos, strings, or flutes. You can hear an instrument, but you feel your heart. And if you think that you feel an instrument, it's only because it touched your heart. Your heart is an instrument made of extremely subtle energy that few people come to appreciate.

In most human beings, the heart does its work unattended. Even though its behavior governs the course of our lives, it is not understood. If at any given point in time the heart happens to open, we fall in love. If at any given point in time it happens to close, the love stops. If the heart happens to hurt, we get angry, and if we stop feeling it altogether, we get empty. All of these different things happen because the heart goes through changes. These energy shifts and variations that take place in the heart run your life. You are so identified with them that you use the words "I" and "me" when you refer to what's going on in your heart. But in truth, you are not your heart. You are the experiencer of your heart.

The heart is actually very simple to understand. It is an energy center, a chakra. It is one of the most beautiful and powerful energy centers, and one that affects our daily lives. As we have seen, an energy center is an area within your being through which your energy focuses, distributes, and flows. This energy flow has been referred to as Shakti, Spirit, and Chi, and it plays an intricate part in your life. You feel the heart's energy all the time. Think about what it is like to feel love in your heart. Think about what it is like to feel inspiration and enthusiasm pour from your heart. Think about what it is like to feel energy well up in your heart making you confident and strong. All of this happens because the heart is an energy center.

The heart controls the energy flow by opening and closing. This means that the heart, like a valve, can either allow the flow of energy to pass through, or it can restrict the flow of energy from passing through. If you observe your heart, you know very well what it feels like when it's open and what it feels like when it's closed. In fact, the state of your heart changes quite regularly. You can be experiencing great feelings of love while in the presence of someone, until they say something you don't like. Then your heart closes toward them, and you simply don't feel the love anymore. We have all experienced this, but what exactly is causing it? Since we all have to experience the heart, we might as well understand what's going on in there.

We begin this analysis by asking a fundamental question: What is it about the structure of the heart center that permits it to close? What you will find is that the heart closes because it becomes blocked by stored, unfinished energy patterns from your past. You need only examine your everyday experiences to understand this. As events take place in this world, they come in through your senses and have an impact on your inner state of being. The experience of these events may bring up some fear, some anxiety, or maybe some love. Different experiences happen inside because of how you take in and digest the world as it passes through you. When you take in the world through your senses, it is actually energy that is coming into your being. Form itself does not come into your mind or heart. Form stays outside, but it is processed by your senses into energy patterns that your mind and heart can receive and experience. Science explains this sensory process to us. Your eyes are not really windows through which you look out into the world. Your eyes are cameras that send electronic images of the world into you. This is true of all your senses. They sense the world, convert the information, transmit the data through electrical nerve impulses, and then the impressions get rendered in your mind. Your senses are, indeed, electronic sensing devices. But if the energy patterns that are coming into your psyche create disturbance, you will resist them and not allow them to pass through you. When you do this, the energy patterns actually get blocked within you.

This is very important. To better understand what it's like to have these energies stored within you, let's first examine what it would be like if nothing was stored. What if everything just passed right through you? For example, when you're driving down a highway, you probably pass thousands of trees. They don't leave impressions on you. They're gone as soon as they're perceived. While you're driving you see trees, you see buildings, you see cars, and none of these make lasting impressions on you. There's just a momentary impression that allows you to see them. Though they do come in through the senses and make impressions upon your mind, as quickly as the impressions are made, they are released. When you have no personal issues with them, impressions process freely.

This is how the overall system of perception is meant to work. It's meant to take things in, allow you to experience them, and then let them pass through so that you're fully present in the next moment. While this system is in a working, operative state, you are fine and it is fine. You're simply having experience after experience. Driving is an experience, trees passing by are an experience, and cars passing by are an experience. These experiences are gifts that are being given to you, like a great movie. They are passing into you, awakening and stimulating you. They are actually having a profound effect on you. Moment after moment, experiences are coming in and you're learning and growing. Your heart and mind are expanding and you are being touched at a very deep level. If experience is the best teacher, there's nothing that comes close to the experience of life.

What it means to live life is to experience the moment that is passing through you, and then experience the next moment, and then the next. Many different experiences will come in and pass through you. It's a phenomenal system when it is working properly. If you could live in that state, you would be a fully aware being. That is how an awakened being lives in the "now." They are present, life is present, and the wholeness of life is passing through them. Imagine if you were so fully present during each experience of life that it was touching you to the depth of your being. Every moment would be a stimulating, moving experience because you would be completely open, and life would be flowing right through you.

But that's not what happens inside most of us. Instead, it's more like you're driving down the street, here come the trees, here come the cars, and it's all passing right through you with no trouble. Then, inevitably, something comes in that doesn't make it through. There was this one car, a light blue Ford Mustang, that looked like your girlfriend's car. But as it passed by, you noticed two people hugging in the front seat. At least it looked like they were hugging, and it sure looked like your girlfriend's car. But it was a car just like all the other cars, wasn't it? No. It wasn't just like all the other cars to you.

Let's look carefully at what happened. Surely for the camera of the eyes there's no difference between that car and the others. There's light bouncing off of objects, passing through your retina, and making a visual impression on your mind. So at the physical level, nothing different is going on. But at the mental level, the impression didn't make it through. When the next moment comes, you no longer notice the rest of the trees. You're not seeing the rest of the cars. Your heart and mind are fixated on that one car, even though it's gone. You've got yourself a problem here. There's a blockage, an event that got stuck. All the subsequent experiences are trying to pass through you, but something has happened inside that has left this past experience unfinished.

What happens to that experience that didn't make it through? Specifically, what happens to the image of the girlfriend's car if it doesn't just fade away into deep memory like everything else? At some point, you'll have to stop focusing on it in order to deal with something else—like the next stoplight. What you don't realize is that your entire experience of life is about to change because of what didn't make it through you. Life must now compete with this blocked event for your attention, and the impression does not just sit in there quietly. You will see that your tendency is to think about it constantly. This is all in an attempt to find a way to process it through your mind. You didn't need to process the trees, but you need to process this. Because you resisted, it got stuck, and now you have a problem. You see the thoughts start up: "Well, maybe it wasn't her. Of course it wasn't her. How could that possibly have been?" Thought after thought goes on inside. It drives you crazy in there. All that inner noise is just your attempt to process the blocked energy and get it out of the way.

Long term, the energy patterns that cannot make it through you are pushed out of the forefront of the mind and held until you are prepared to release them. These energy patterns, which hold tremendous detail about the events associated with them, are real. They don't just disappear. When you are unable to allow life's events to pass through you, they stay inside and become a problem. These patterns may be held within you for a very long time.

It is not easy to keep energy together in one place for long. As you willfully struggle to keep these events from passing through your consciousness, the energy first tries to release by manifesting through the mind. This is why the mind becomes so active. When the energy can't make it through the mind because of conflicts with other thoughts and mental concepts, it then tries to release through the heart. That is what creates all the emotional activity. When you resist even that release, the energy gets packed up and forced into deep storage within the heart. In the yogic tradition, that unfinished energy pattern is called a *Samskara*. This is a Sanskrit word meaning "impression," and in the yogic teachings it is considered one of the most important influences affecting your life. A Samskara is a blockage, an impression from the past. It's an unfinished energy pattern that ends up running your life.

In order to understand this, let's first take an indepth look at the physics behind these blocked energy patterns. Just like energy waves, the energy that comes into you must keep moving. But that doesn't mean it can't get blocked within you. There is a way that the energy can both keep moving and stay in one place—and that is to circle around itself. We see this in atoms and in planetary orbits. Everything is energy, and energy will just expand outward if it is not contained. For there to be manifest creation, energy must get in the dynamic of cycling around itself to create a stable unit. That's why energy manifesting as an atom forms the basic building block of this entire physical universe. Energy cycles around itself, and as we've discovered, atoms have enough harnessed energy to blow up the world when that energy is released. But unless forced otherwise, the energy will stay harnessed because of its equilibrium state.

This process of cycling energy is exactly what happens with a Samskara. A Samskara is a cycle of stored past energy patterns in a state of relative equilibrium. It is your resistance to experiencing these patterns that causes the energy to keep cycling around itself. There is no other place for it to go. You won't let it. This is how most people process their issues. This packet of cycling energy is literally stored in your energetic heart center. All the Samskaras you have collected over your life are stored there.

To fully appreciate what this means, let's go back to the example of the light blue Mustang that looked like your girlfriend's car. Once the disturbed energy patterns are packaged and stored in the heart, they are basically inactive. It may look to you like you have handled the situation and that you have no more issues with that experience. You may not even mention the event to your girlfriend because it would look like you were jealous. You didn't know what to do, so you resisted the energy, and it got stored in the heart where it could fall into the background and not be bothersome. While it may seem like it's done, like it is all over and gone, it really isn't.

Every one of the Samskaras that you've stored is still there. Everything that did not make it through you, from the time you were a baby all the way to this moment, is still inside of you. It is these impressions, these Samskaras, that encrust the valve of the spiritual heart. That encrustation builds up and restricts the energy flow.

Now that we understand where the blockages within the heart come from, we have answered the structural question of how the heart gets blocked. You can certainly see the potential for impressions to build up to the point where very little energy can make it through. If they build up sufficiently, you will find yourself in a state of depression. In that state, all becomes dark. This is because very little energy is coming into your heart or mind. Eventually, everything appears negative because the world of the senses must pass through this depressed energy before it gets to your consciousness.

But even if you aren't prone to depression, your heart still gets blocked over time. It just builds up. It doesn't always stay blocked, however. Depending upon life's experiences, it can open and close quite frequently. This leads us to our next question: What is the cause of these frequent changes in the state of the heart? If you watch carefully, you will see it is related to the same stored past impressions that caused the blockages.

The stored energy patterns are real. A Samskara is actually programmed with the specific details of the event that could not pass through. If you experience jealousy because you thought you saw your girlfriend hugging someone in a car, very detailed data about that event is stored in the Samskara. It has that event's vibration, it has that event's nature, and it even retains your level of sensitivity about the event.

To see this, let's watch what happens in the future. It's five years later and you're no longer with your old girlfriend. You've married someone else and you're much more mature. One day you're out driving along with the family having a wonderful time. The trees are going by, the cars are going by, and then a light blue Mustang drives by with two people hugging in the front seat. Immediately, something changes in your heart. Your heart actually skips a beat. Then it starts beating faster. You start getting moody, irritated, and agitated. You aren't having such a nice day anymore. All of these inner changes occur because your heart got disturbed when you saw one particular car. It is truly amazing to step back and look at this process. Five years ago, for just a few moments, an event took place. You never discussed it with anybody, and now five years later, a light blue Mustang drives by and it changes the energy flow through your heart and mind.

As unbelievable as this seems, it is true. And it's not only true about light blue Mustangs; it's true about everything that didn't make it through you. No wonder we're so overwhelmed. No wonder the heart keeps opening and closing. The energy that's stored there is real, and it interacts with the flow of current thoughts and events. The dynamics of this interaction cause the vibrations that are stored as Samskaras to get activated, sometimes years later. This is what happened with the light blue Mustang. Understand, however, that it didn't even have to be the identical car to activate the stored energy. It could have been a black Mustang or any car with people hugging. Anything in the neighborhood has the potential to stimulate a Samskara.

The point is that past impressions do get stimulated, even old ones, and they affect your life. Sensory inputs from today's events dig through all the stuff you have stored through the years, and they restore the exact past patterns associated with the incoming events. When a Samskara is stimulated, it opens like a flower and begins to release the stored energy. Suddenly, flashes of what you experienced when the original event took place rush into your consciousness—the thoughts, the feelings, sometimes even the smells and other sensory input. The Samskara can store a complete snapshot of the event. It is way beyond any computer storage system created by human beings. It can archive everything you were feeling, everything you were thinking, and everything that was happening surrounding the event. All this information is stored into a tiny energy bubble within your heart. Years later it gets stimulated, and instantly you are experiencing the feelings you felt in the past. You can actually feel the fears and the insecurity of a five-year-old when you're sixty. What is happening is that unfinished mental and emotional energy patterns are getting stored and reactivated.

But it is just as important to realize that most of what you take in does not get blocked; it makes it right through you. Imagine how many things you see all day. They're not all stored like that. Of all these impressions, the only ones that get blocked are those that cause either problems or some extraordinary sense of enjoyment. Yes, you store positive impressions too. When a wonderful experience happens to you, it doesn't make it through because you cling to it. Clinging means "I don't want this one to go away. He told me he loved me and I felt so loved and protected. I want to keep reliving that moment. Play it back for me over and over again…" Clinging creates positive Samskaras, and when these are stimulated, they release positive energy. Hence two kinds of experiences can occur that block the heart. You are either trying to push energies away because they bother you, or you are trying to keep energies close because you like them. In both cases, you are not letting them pass, and you are wasting precious energy by blocking the flow through resisting and clinging.

The alternative is to enjoy life instead of clinging to it or pushing it away. If you can live like that, each moment will change you. If you are willing to experience the gift of life instead of fighting with it, you will be moved to the depth of your being. When you reach this state, you will begin to see the secrets of the heart. The heart is the place through which energy flows to sustain you. This energy inspires you and raises you. It is the strength that carries you through life. It is the beautiful experience of love that pours through your whole being. This is meant to be going on inside you at all times. The highest state you have ever experienced is simply the result of how open you were. If you don't close, it can be like that all the time. Don't sell yourself short. This can go on all the time—unending inspiration, unending love, and unending openness. That is the natural state of a healthy heart.

To achieve this state, simply allow the experiences of life to come in and pass through your being. If old energies come back up because you were unable to process them before, let go of them now. It's that easy. When that light blue Mustang drives by and you feel fear or jealousy, just smile. Be happy that this Samskara, which has been stored down there for all this time, has the opportunity to make it through you. Just open, relax your heart, forgive, laugh, or do anything you want. Just don't push it back down. Of course it hurts when it comes up. It was stored with pain; it's going to release with pain. You have to decide if you want to continue to walk around with stored pain blocking your heart and limiting your life. The alternative is to be willing to let it go when it gets stimulated. It only hurts for a minute and then it's over.

So, you have a choice: Do you want to try to change the world so it doesn't disturb your Samskaras, or are you willing to go through this process of purification? Don't make decisions based on stimulated blockages. Learn to be centered enough to just watch this stuff come up. Once you sit deeply enough inside to stop fighting the stored energy patterns, they'll come up constantly and pass right through you. They'll come up during the day and they'll even come up in your dreams. Your heart will become accustomed to the process of releasing and cleansing. Just let it all happen. Get it over with. Don't process them one by one; that's too slow. Stay centered behind them and let go. Just like the physical body purges bacteria and other foreign matter, the natural flow of your energy will purge the stored patterns from your heart.

Your reward is a permanently open heart. There is no more valve. You live in love, and it feeds you and strengthens you. That is an open heart. That is the instrument of the heart as it was meant to be. Allow yourself to experience every note the heart can play. If you relax and release, this purification of your heart is a wonderful thing. Set your eyes on the highest state you can imagine and don't take them off. If you slip, just get back up. It doesn't matter. The very fact that you even want to go through this process of freeing the energy flow means you are great. You will get there. Just keep letting go.

CHAPTER 7

transcending the tendency to close

The foundations of spiritual growth and personal awakening are very much strengthened by the findings of Western science. Science has shown us how an underlying energy field forms into atoms, which then bind together into molecules, and ultimately manifest into the entire physical universe. The same is true inside of us. All that goes on inside also has its foundation in an underlying energy field. It is the movements in this field that create our mental and emotional patterns as well as our inner drives, urges, and instinctual reactions. Regardless of what you call this inner force field—Chi, Shakti, or Spirit—it is an underlying energy that flows in particular patterns through your inner being.

When looking at these patterns within yourself, as well as in other living species, it is not difficult to see that the most primal energy flow is the survival instinct. During eons of evolution, from the simplest of living forms to the most complex, there has always been the day-to-day struggle to protect oneself. In our highly evolved cooperative social structures, this survival instinct has gone through evolutionary changes. Many of us no longer lack food, water, clothing, or shelter; nor do we regularly face life-threatening physical danger. As a result, the protective energies have adapted toward defending the individual psychologically, rather than physiologically. We now experience the daily need to defend our self-concepts rather than our bodies. Our major struggles end up being with our own inner fears, insecurities, and destructive behavior patterns, and not with outside forces.

Nonetheless, the same impulses that make a deer run away urge you to run away. Suppose somebody raises their voice at you or talks about an uncomfortable subject. These are not physically threatening circumstances, yet your heart starts pumping a little faster. That's exactly what happens to deer whenever they hear a sudden sound. Their hearts start pumping faster, and they either freeze or run away. In your case, however, it's not usually the kind of fear that causes you to physically run away. It's just a deep, personal fear demanding protection.

Since it's not socially acceptable to run into the woods and hide like a deer, you hide inside. You withdraw, close down, and pull back behind your protective shield. What you are actually doing is closing down your energy centers. Even if you don't know you have energy centers, you've been closing them since kindergarten. You know exactly how to close your heart and put up a psychological protective shield. You know exactly how to close down the centers to avoid being too receptive and sensitive to the different energies coming in and causing fear.

When you close down and protect yourself, you are pulling a shell around the part of you that is weak. This is the part that feels it needs protection even though no physical attack is taking place. You are protecting your ego, your self-concept. Although a situation may present no physical danger, it may cause you to experience disturbance, fear, insecurity, and other emotional problems. So you feel the need to protect yourself.

The problem is that the part of you that gets disturbed is way out of balance. It's so sensitive that the slightest little thing causes it to overreact. You are living on a planet spinning around the middle of outer space, and you're either worrying about your blemishes, the scratch on your new car, or the fact that you burped in public. It's not healthy. If your physical body were that sensitive, you would say you were sick. But our society considers psychological sensitivities normal. Because most of us don't have to worry about food, clothing, or shelter, we have the luxury of worrying about a spot on our pants, or laughing too loud, or saying something wrong. Because we've developed this hypersensitive psyche, we constantly use our energies to close around it and protect ourselves. But this process only hides the problems; it doesn't fix them. You're locking your illness inside yourself, and it will only get worse.

Transcending the Tendency to Close

You will get to a point in your growth where you understand that if you protect yourself, you will never be free. It's that simple. Because you're scared, you have locked yourself within your house and pulled down all the shades. Now it's dark and you want to feel the sunlight, but you can't. It's impossible. If you close and protect yourself, you are locking this scared, insecure person within your heart. You will never be free that way.

Ultimately, if you protect yourself perfectly, you will never grow. All your habits and idiosyncrasies will stay the same. Life becomes stagnant when people protect their stored issues. People say things like, "You know we don't talk about that subject around your father." There are all these rules about things that are not supposed to happen outside because they could cause disturbance inside. Living like this allows for very little spontaneous joy, enthusiasm, and excitement for life. Most people just go from day to day protecting themselves and making sure nothing goes too wrong. At the end of the day, when someone asks, "How was your day?" a normal response is, "Not too bad," or "I'll survive." What is that telling you about their view of life? They see life as a threat. A good day means you made it through without getting hurt. The longer you live like this, the more closed you become.

If you really want to grow, you have to do the opposite. Real spiritual growth happens when there is only one of you inside. There's not a part that's scared and another part that's protecting the part that's scared. All parts are unified. Because there is no part of you that you're not willing to see, the mind is no longer divided into the conscious and subconscious. Everything you see inside is just something you see inside. It's not you; it's what you see. There is simply the pure energy pouring inside of you that creates the ripples of thoughts and emotions, and there is the consciousness that's aware of it. There is simply you watching the dance of the psyche.

In order to reach this state of awareness, you must let your entire psyche surface. Every little separated piece of it must be permitted to pass through. Right now, many fragmented parts of your psyche are held within you. If you want to be free, it all has to be equally exposed to your awareness and released. But it will never get exposed if you're closing yourself. After all, the purpose of closing was to make sure that the sensitive parts of your psyche don't get exposed. So you catch on that no matter how much pain the exposure creates, you are willing to pay that price for freedom. When you are no longer willing to identify with the part of you that is separating itself into a million pieces, you are ready for real growth.

Transcending the Tendency to Close

Begin by seeing the tendency to protect and defend yourself. There is a very deep, innate tendency to close, especially around your soft spots. But eventually you will notice that closing creates tremendous work. Once you close, you have to make sure that what you protected doesn't get disturbed. You then carry this task for the rest of your life. The alternative is to become conscious enough to simply watch the part of your being that is constantly trying to protect itself. You can then give yourself the ultimate gift by deciding not to do that anymore. You decide, instead, to get rid of that part.

You start by watching life and noticing the constant flow of people and situations that hit your stuff every day. How often do you find yourself trying to protect and defend that weak part of you? You feel like the world wants to get right at it. Every place you go there's someone or something trying to disturb you, trying to get your goat. Why not let them have it? If you don't really want it, then don't protect it.

The reward for not protecting your psyche is liberation. You are free to walk through this world without a problem on your mind. You are just having fun experiencing whatever happens next. Because you got rid of that scared part of you, you don't ever have to worry about getting hurt or disturbed. You no longer have to listen to "What will they think of me?" or, "Oh God, I wish I hadn't said that. It sounded so stupid." You just go about your business and put your whole being into whatever's happening, instead of putting your whole being into your personal sensitivity.

Once you've made the commitment to free yourself of that scared person inside, you will notice that there is a clear decision point at which your growth takes place. Spiritual growth is about the point at which you start to feel your energy change. For instance, somebody says something, and you start to feel the energy get a little strange inside. You will actually start to feel a tightening. That is your cue that it's time to grow. It's not time to defend yourself, because you don't want the part of you that you would be defending. If you don't want it, let it go.

You will eventually get conscious enough so that the minute you see the energy start getting strange, you stop. You stop getting involved in the energy. If it normally causes you to start talking, you stop talking. You just stop, mid-sentence, because you know where it will go if you continue. The moment you see the energy getting imbalanced inside, the moment you see the heart starting to tense and get defensive, you just stop.

What exactly does it mean "to stop"? It's something you do inside. It's called letting go. When you let go, you are falling behind the energy that is trying to pull you into it. Your energies inside have power. They are very strong, and they draw your awareness into them. If a hammer falls on your toe, all your awareness will focus there. If there's a sudden loud sound, again, all of your awareness will focus there. Consciousness has the tendency to focus on disturbance, and disturbed energies inside are no exception. These disturbed energies will draw your consciousness to them. But you do not have to let this happen. You really do have the ability to disengage and fall back behind them.

When the energies inside start to move, you do not have to go there. For instance, when your thoughts start, you do not have to go with them. Let's say you're outside taking a walk and a car drives by. Your thoughts say, "Boy, I wish I had that car." You could just keep on walking, but instead you start getting upset. You want a car like that, but your salary isn't high enough. So you begin thinking about how you can get a raise or a different job. You didn't have to do all that. It could have just been—here comes the car and there it goes, and here comes the thought and there it goes. They're both gone together because you didn't go with them. That is what's called being centered.

If you aren't centered, your consciousness is just following whatever catches its attention. You see the car drive by and you're off doing something about it. Another day you see a boat, and then it is all about the boat, and you forget about the car. There are people like that. They don't hold jobs very well and relationships don't tend to work out for them. They're just all over the place; their energy is very scattered.

You have the ability to not go with any of these thoughts. You can just sit in the seat of consciousness and let go. A thought or emotion emerges, you notice it, and it passes by because you allow it to. This technique of freeing yourself is done with the understanding that thoughts and emotions are just objects of consciousness. When you see your heart start getting anxious, you are obviously aware of this experience. But who is aware? It is the consciousness, the indwelling being, the Soul, the Self. It is the seer, the one who sees. The changes you experience in your inner energy flow are simply objects of this consciousness. If you want to be free, then every time you feel any change in the energy flow, relax behind it. Don't fight with it, don't try to change it, and don't judge it. Don't say, "Oh, I can't believe I'm still feeling this. I promised myself I wouldn't think about that car anymore." Don't do that; you'll just end up going with the guilt thoughts instead of the car thoughts. You have to let them all go.

But it's not just about letting go of thoughts and emotions. It's actually about letting go of the pull that the energy itself has on your consciousness. The disturbed energy is trying to draw your attention into it. If you use your inner willpower to not go with it, and just remain seated within, you will notice that the distinction between the consciousness and the object of consciousness is like night and day. They are totally different things. The object comes and goes, and the consciousness watches it come and go. Then the next object comes and goes while the consciousness watches it. Both objects came and went, but the consciousness didn't go anywhere. It stays constant and simply watches all of it. The consciousness experiences the creation of thoughts and emotions, and it has the clarity to see where they came from. It sees all of this without thinking about it. It sees what's going on inside as easily as it sees what's going on outside. It simply watches. The Self is watching the inside energies change in accordance to both inside and outside forces. All the energies that it watches will just come and go, unless you lose your center of consciousness and go with them.

Let's take a slow-motion look at what happens if you go with these energies. First, you start to have a thought or feeling. This feeling could be as subtle as your energy flow starting to tighten and become defensive, or it could be something much stronger. If these energies capture your consciousness and all the power of awareness gets focused on them, this power actually feeds them. Consciousness is a tremendously powerful force. When you concentrate on these thoughts and emotions, they become charged with energy and power. This is why thoughts and emotions get stronger the more attention you give them. Let's say you feel a little jealousy or a little fear. If you focus on it, it grows in importance and demands more of your attention. Then, because your attention feeds it, it becomes infused with even more energy and draws more attention. That's how the cycle goes. Eventually, what started as a passing thought or emotion can become the center of your entire life. If you don't let go, it can get completely out of control.

A wise person remains centered enough to let go every time the energy shifts into a defensive mode. The moment the energy moves and you feel your consciousness start to get drawn into it, you relax and release. Letting go means falling behind the energy instead of going into it. It just takes a moment of conscious effort to decide that you're not going there. You just let go. It's simply a matter of taking the risk that you are better off letting go than going with the energy. When you're free from the hold the energy has on you, you will be free to experience the joy and expansiveness that exists within you.

So you decide to use life to free yourself. You become willing to pay any price for the freedom of your soul. You will realize that the only price you have to pay is letting go of yourself. Only you can take inner freedom away from yourself, or give it to yourself. Nobody else can. It doesn't matter what others do, unless you decide that it matters to you. Begin with small things. We tend to let ourselves get bothered by the little, meaningless things that happen every day. For example, somebody beeps at you at the stoplight. As these little things happen, you will feel your energy change. The moment you feel a change, relax your shoulders and relax the area around your heart. The moment the energy moves, you simply relax and release. Play with letting go and falling behind this sense of being bothered. Let's say someone at work took your pencil, and you notice that every time you go to use another one, your inner energy shifts—even the slightest amount. Are you willing to release the old pencil in order to liberate yourself? This is how you make freedom a game. Instead of getting into being bothered, you get into being free. When you reach for a pencil, and you see yourself getting a little uptight, let go. Your mind might start saying, "It was a pencil today and if I let go, they'll step all over me. It'll be my desk tomorrow, or my house, or maybe even my husband." That's how the mind talks. It's very melodramatic. But you decide

105

that for the cost of a pencil, you'll go for the ride. You tell your mind, "When it's the car, we'll have a talk. Right now, it only costs a pencil to be free." Just decide that no matter what the mind says, you aren't getting involved. You don't fight the mind. In fact, you don't even try to change it. You just make a game out of relaxing in the face of its melodrama. You simply learn how to release the tendency for getting drawn into the energy. The root is where the consciousness is aware of the pull of these energies.

You will see that the energy does have the power to draw you in. Even once you decide you're not going to let this happen, it still has a tremendous power over you. It happens at work and it happens at home. It happens with your children and with your husband or wife. It happens with everything and everybody all the time. Your opportunities to grow are endless. It's always there in front of you. Just commit to not letting the energy draw you in. When you feel the pull, like somebody pulling on your heart, you just let go. You fall behind it. You simply relax and release. And no matter how many times you're pulled, that's how many times you relax and release. Because the tendency to get drawn in is constant, the willingness to let go and fall behind has to be constant.

Your center of consciousness is always stronger than the energy that is pulling on it. You just have to be willing to exercise your will. But it's not a fight or a struggle. It's not that you are trying to stop the energies from coming up inside. There is nothing wrong with feeling the energies of fear, jealousy, or attraction. It's not your fault that such energies exist. All the attractions, repulsions, thoughts, and feelings don't make any difference. They don't make you pure or impure. They are not you. You are the one who's watching, and that one is pure consciousness. Don't think you'd be free if you just didn't have these kinds of feelings. It's not true. If you can be free even though you're having these kinds of feelings, then you're really free—because there will always be something.

If you can learn to remain centered with the smaller things, you will see that you can also remain centered with bigger things. Over time, you will find that you can even remain centered with the really big things. The types of events that would have destroyed you in the past can come and go, leaving you perfectly centered and peaceful. You can be fine, deep inside, even in the face of a deep sense of loss. There's nothing wrong with being peaceful and centered as long as you are releasing the energy, not suppressing it. Ultimately, even if terrible things happen, you should be able to live without emotional scars and impressions. If you don't hold these issues inside, you can go about your life without getting psychologically damaged. No matter what events take place in life, it is always better to let go rather than to close.

There's a place deep inside of you where the consciousness touches the energy, and the energy touches the consciousness. That's where your work is. From that place, you let go. Once you've let go, every minute of every day, year after year, then that's where you'll live. Nothing will be able to take your seat of consciousness from you. You'll learn to stay there. After you've put years and years into this process, and learned to let go no matter how deep the pain, you will achieve a great state. You will break the ultimate habit: the constant draw of the lower self. You will then be free to explore the nature and source of your true being—Pure Consciousness.

PART III

freeing yourself

CHAPTER 8

let go now or fall

The exploration of Self is inextricably interwoven with the unfolding of one's life. The natural ups and downs of life can either generate personal growth or create personal fears. Which of these dominates is completely dependent upon how we view change. Change can be viewed as either exciting or frightening, but regardless of how we view it, we must all face the fact that change is the very nature of life. If you have a lot of fear, you won't like change. You'll try to create a world around you that is predictable, controllable, and definable. You'll try to create a world that doesn't stimulate your fears. Fear doesn't want to feel itself; it's actually afraid of itself. So you utilize the mind in an attempt to manipulate life for the purpose of not feeling fear.

People don't understand that fear is a thing. It's just another object in the universe that you are capable of experiencing. You can do one of two things with fear: you can recognize that you have it and work to release it, or you can keep it and try to hide from it. Because people don't deal with fear objectively, they don't understand it. They end up keeping their fear and trying to prevent things from happening that would stimulate it. They go through life attempting to create safety and control by defining how they need life to be in order to be okay. This is how the world becomes frightening.

This may not sound frightening; it may sound safe. But it's not. If you do this, the world truly becomes threatening. Life becomes a "me against it" situation. When you have fear, insecurity, or weakness inside of you, and you attempt to keep it from being stimulated, there will inevitably be events and changes in life that challenge your efforts. Because you resist these changes, you feel that you are struggling with life. You feel like this person is not behaving the way they should, and this event is not unfolding the way you want. You see situations that happened in the past as disturbing, and you see things down the road as potential problems. Your definitions of desirable and undesirable, as well as good and bad, all come about because you have defined how things need to be in order for you to be okay.

We all know that we're doing this, but nobody questions it. We think we're supposed to figure out how life should be, and then make it that way. Only someone who looks deeper, and questions why we need the events of life to be a particular way, will question this assumption. How did we come up with the notion that life is not okay just the way it is, or that it won't be okay the way it will be? Who said that the way life naturally unfolds is not all right?

The answer is, fear says so. The part of you inside that's not okay with itself can't face the natural unfolding of life because it's not under your control. If life unfolds in a way that stimulates your inner problems, then, by definition, it's not okay. It's really very simple: that which doesn't disturb you is okay, and that which does disturb you is not. We define the entire scope of our outer experience based upon our inner problems. If you want to grow spiritually, you have to change that. If you are defining creation based upon the most messed up part of your being, what do you expect creation to look like? It's going to look like a frightful mess.

As you grow spiritually, you will realize that your attempts to protect yourself from your problems actually create more problems. If you attempt to arrange people, places, and things so they don't disturb you, it will begin to feel like life is against you. You'll feel that life is a struggle and that every day is heavy because you have to control and fight with everything. There will be competition, jealousy, and fear. You will feel that anyone, at any moment, could cause you disturbance. All they have to do is say or do one thing, and the next thing you know there's disturbance inside of you. That makes life a threat. That's why you have to worry so much. That's why you have all these dialogues going on inside your mind. You're either trying to figure out how to keep things from happening, or you're trying to figure out what to do because they did happen. You are fighting with creation, and that's what makes creation itself the most frightening thing in your life.

The alternative is to decide not to fight with life. You realize and accept that life is not under your control. Life is continuously changing, and if you're trying to control it, you'll never be able to fully live it. Instead of living life, you'll be afraid of life. But once you've decided not to fight with life, you'll have to face the fear that was causing you to fight. Fortunately, you don't have to keep this fear inside of you. There is such a thing as a life without fear. In order to relate to this possibility, we must first have a deeper understanding of fear itself.

When you have fear inside of you, the events of life invariably stimulate it. Like a rock thrown into water, the world with its continuous changes creates ripples in whatever is held within you. There's nothing wrong with that. Life creates situations that push you to your edges, all with the effect of removing what is blocked inside of you. That which is blocked and buried within you forms the root of fear. Fear is caused by blockages in the flow of your energy. When your energy is blocked, it can't come up and feed your heart. Therefore, your heart becomes weak. When your heart is weak it becomes susceptible to lower vibrations, and one of the lowest of all vibrations is fear. Fear is the cause of every problem. It's the root of all prejudices and the negative emotions of anger, jealousy, and possessiveness. If you had no fear, you could be perfectly happy living in this world. Nothing would bother you. You'd be willing to face everything and everyone because you wouldn't have fear inside of you that could cause you disturbance.

The purpose of spiritual evolution is to remove the blockages that cause your fear. The alternative is to protect your blockages so that you don't have to feel fear. To do this, however, you will have to try to control everything in order to avoid your inner issues. It's hard to understand how we decided that avoiding our inner issues is an intelligent thing to do, but everybody's doing it. Everyone is saying, "I will do every single thing I can to keep my stuff. If you say anything that disturbs me, I will defend myself. I'll yell at you and make you take it back. If you cause any disturbance inside of me, I will make you so sorry." In other words, if somebody does something that stimulates fear, you think they did something wrong. You then do everything you can to make sure they never do it again. First you defend yourself, and then you protect yourself. You do whatever you can to keep from feeling disturbance.

Eventually, you become wise enough to realize that you do not want that stuff inside of you. It doesn't matter who stimulates it. It doesn't matter what situation hits it. It doesn't matter whether it makes sense, or whether it seems fair or not. Unfortunately, most of us are not that wise. We're really not trying to be free of our stuff; we're trying to justify keeping it.

If you truly want to grow spiritually, you'll realize that keeping your stuff is keeping you trapped. Eventually you'll want out, at any cost. You will then realize that life is actually trying to help you. Life is surrounding you with people and situations that stimulate growth. You don't have to decide who's right or wrong. You don't have to worry about other people's issues. You only have to be willing to open your heart in the face of anything and everything, and permit the purification process to take place. When you do this, the first thing you'll see is that situations will unfold that hit your stuff. But, in truth, that's exactly what has been happening your entire life. The only difference is that now you see it as a good thing because it's an opportunity to let go.

The stuff that holds you down periodically rears its head. When it does, let it go. You simply permit the pain to come up into your heart and pass through. If you do that, it will pass. If you are sincerely seeking truth, you'll let go every time. This is the beginning and end of the entire path—you surrender yourself to the process of emptying yourself. When you work with this, you start to learn the subtler laws of the process of letting go.

There is a law you will learn very early in the game because it is an unavoidable truth. You will learn it early, but you will fall many times while trying to adhere to it. The law is very straightforward: When your stuff gets hit, let go right then because it will be harder later. It won't be easier if you explore it or play with it, hoping to take the edge off. It won't be easier to think about it, talk about it, or try to release only part of it at a time. If you want to be free to the core of your being, you must let go right away because it will not be easier later.

In order to live by this law, you have to understand its principles. First, you must be aware that there is something within you that needs to be released. You must then be aware that you, the one who notices the stuff coming up, are distinct from what you're experiencing. You are noticing it, but who are you? This place of centered awareness is the seat of the witness, the seat of Self. That is the only seat from which you can let go. Let's say you notice that something in your heart gets hit. If you let go and stay in the seat of awareness, what you are noticing will pass. If you don't let go, and instead get lost in the disturbed feelings and thoughts that arise, you'll see a sequence of events unfold so quickly you won't know what hit you.

If you don't let go, you'll notice that the energy that got stimulated in your heart works like a magnet. It's a phenomenally attractive force that will pull your consciousness into it. The next thing you know, you won't be there. You won't maintain the same perspective of awareness that you had when you first noticed the disturbance. You will leave the seat of objective awareness from which you saw your heart begin to react, and you will get involved in the shifting energies coming from your heart. Some time later you'll come back and realize you weren't there. You'll come back and realize that you were totally lost in your stuff. Then you will hope that you didn't say or do anything you'll regret.

You'll look at the clock, and five minutes will have gone by, or an hour, or even a year. You can lose your clarity for quite some time. Where did you go? How did you come back? We will address these questions shortly, but what really matters is that when you're seeing clearly, you're not going anywhere. You're simply sitting in the seat of centered awareness watching your stuff get hit. As long as you're watching, you're not getting lost in it.

The key is to understand that if you don't let go immediately, the disturbing force of the activated energy draws the focus of your consciousness. As your consciousness gets immersed in the disturbance, you lose your clear seat of Self. It happens instantaneously. There's no feeling of going anywhere, any more than there is when you leave the room by getting absorbed in a book or TV show. You simply lose the fixed point of consciousness from which you were objectively aware of your surroundings. Your consciousness leaves the centered position of witnessing the many energies around you, and you get sucked into focusing on just one of them.

This leaving the seat of Self is not generally a willful act. The laws of attraction will cause it to happen. Consciousness is always drawn to the most distracting object: the bumped toe, the loud noise, or the hurting heart. It's the same law, both inside and out. The consciousness goes to the place that distracts it the most. That's what we mean when we say, "It was so loud it caught my attention." It drew your consciousness to it. When a blockage gets hit, this same attraction takes place, and the consciousness gets pulled to the source of discomfort. That place then becomes your seat of consciousness. After the discomfort settles down and lets you go, you'll naturally drift back toward your higher seat of awareness. This is where you sit when you're not distracted by disturbance. But as important as this higher seat is, it is equally important to see what happens when you are distracted by disturbance—your seat of consciousness falls down to where the disturbance is happening, and the whole world looks different.

Let's analyze this fall, step by step. It begins when you get pulled down into the disturbed energy. You end up exactly where you don't belong. The last place you want to put your consciousness is down there. But that's where it will get pulled. Now, as you look out through your disturbed energy, everything is distorted by the haze of your disturbance. Things that looked beautiful now look ugly. Things you liked, now look dark and depressing. But nothing has really changed. It's just that you're looking at life from that seat of disturbance.

Each of these shifts in your perception should remind you to let go. The moment you start seeing that you don't like the people you used to like, the moment you start seeing that your life looks really different, the moment it all starts getting negative—let go. You should have let go before, but you didn't. The trouble is that it's more difficult now. You could have taken one breath and let go when it started. Now it takes serious work to get your previous seat of consciousness back without going through the whole cycle.

The cycle is the time it takes from the moment you leave your seat of relative clarity until you come back. This period of time is determined by the depth of the energy blockage that caused the initial disturbance. Once activated, the blockage must run its course. If you don't let go, you get sucked in. You are no longer free; you are caught. Once you fall from your seat of relative clarity, you are under the mercy of the disturbed energy.

If that blockage is stimulated by an ongoing situation, you may stay down there for a long time. If it happens to be just a passing event, and the energy released by the blockage dissipates immediately, then you'll find that you drift back up quickly. The main point is that it's not under your control. You lost it.

This is the anatomy of falling. When you're in this state of disturbance, your tendency will be to act in order to try to fix things. You don't have the clarity to see what's going on; you just want the disturbance to stop. So you start getting down to your survival instincts. You may feel that you have to do something drastic. You may want to leave your husband or wife, or move, or quit your job. The mind starts saying all kinds of things because it doesn't like this space, and it wants to get away from it any way it can.

Now that you've fallen to that point, here comes the crème de la crème. Imagine that while you're lost in the disturbed energy, you actually do one or more of the things that your mind is telling you to do. Imagine what would happen if you actually quit your job, or if you decide, "I've held this in long enough. I'm going to give him a piece of my mind." You have no idea how big a step down that is. It's one thing if the disturbance is going on inside of you. But the moment you allow it to express itself, the moment you let that energy move your body, you have descended to another level. Now it's almost impossible to let go. If you start yelling at somebody, if you actually tell someone how you feel about them from this state of nonclarity, you have involved that person's heart and mind in your stuff. Now both of your egos are involved. Once you externalize these energies, you will want to defend your actions and make them look appropriate. But the other person will never think they were appropriate.

Now even more forces are keeping you down. First you fall into the darkness, and then you manifest that darkness. When you do this, you are literally taking the energy of the blockage and passing it on. When you dump your stuff into this world, it's like painting the world with your stuff. You put more of that kind of energy into your environment and it comes back to you. You are now surrounded by people who will interact with you accordingly. It's just another form of "environmental pollution," and it will affect your life.

That is how negative cycles happen. You actually take a piece of your stuff, which is nothing but deeply seated disturbance from your past, and you implant it in the hearts of those around you. At some point it will come back to you. Anything you put out comes back. Imagine if you got upset and fully released your disturbed energies onto another person. This is how people ruin relationships and destroy their lives.

How far down can you go? Once you're weakened, another blockage could get hit, and yet another. You can fall all the way down until your life is an absolute mess. You can reach a point of total loss of control and completely lose your center. In this state, your previous seat of clarity may drift by once in a while, but you can't hold it. Now you're lost. Do you doubt that a single blockage getting hit in your heart could cause a fall that lasts a lifetime? It has been known to happen.

What if all you had to do to avoid all of this was to let go in the beginning? If you had, you would have gone up instead of down. That's how it works. When a blockage gets hit, it's a good thing. It's time to open up internally and release the blocked energy. If you let go, and permit the purification process to take place inside, that blocked energy will be released. When it's released and allowed to flow up, it becomes purified and merges back into your center of consciousness. This energy then strengthens you instead of weakening you. You begin to go up and up, higher and higher, and you learn the secret of the ascent. The secret of the ascent is to never look down—always look up.

No matter what happens below you, just turn your eyes upward and relax your heart. You do not have to leave the seat of Self in order to deal with the darkness. It will purify itself if you let it. Getting involved in the darkness does not dispel darkness; it feeds it. Don't even turn toward it. If you see disturbed energies within you, it's okay. Don't think that you don't have blockages left to release. Just sit in the seat of awareness and never leave. No matter what goes on below you, open your heart and let it go. Your heart will become purified, and you will never know another fall.

If you fall along the way, just get up and forget it. Use the lesson to strengthen your resolve. Let go right then. Do not rationalize, blame, or try to figure it out. Don't do anything. Just let go immediately, and allow the energy to go back to the highest center of consciousness it can achieve. If you feel shame, let it go. If you feel fear, let it go. All of these are the remnants of the blocked energy that is finally being purified.

Always let go as soon as you're aware that you didn't. Don't waste your time; use the energy to go up. You are a great being who has been given a tremendous opportunity to explore beyond yourself. The whole process is very exciting, and you will have good times and bad times. All sorts of things will happen. That's the fun of the journey.

So don't fall. Let go. No matter what it is, let it go. The bigger it is, the higher the reward of letting go and the worse the fall if you don't. It's pretty black-and-white. You either let go or you don't. There really isn't anything in between. So let all of your blockages and disturbances become the fuel for the journey. That which is holding you down can become a powerful force that raises you up. You just have to be willing to take the ascent.

CHAPTER 9

removing your inner thorn

The spiritual journey is one of constant transformation. In order to grow, you must give up the struggle to remain the same, and learn to embrace change at all times. One of the most important areas requiring change is how we solve our personal problems. We normally attempt to solve our inner disturbances by protecting ourselves. Real transformation begins when you embrace your problems as agents for growth. In order to understand how this process works, let's examine the following situation.

Imagine that you have a thorn in your arm that directly touches a nerve. When the thorn is touched, it's very painful. Because it hurts so much, the thorn is a serious problem. It's difficult to sleep because you roll over on it. It's hard to get close to people because they might touch it. It makes your daily life very difficult. You can't even go for a walk in the woods because you might brush the thorn against the branches. This thorn is a constant source of disturbance, and to solve the problem you only have two choices.

The first choice is to look at your situation and decide that since it's so disturbing when things touch the thorn, you need to make sure nothing touches it. The second choice is to decide that since it's so disturbing when things touch the thorn, you need to take it out. Believe it or not, the effects of the choice you make will determine the course of the rest of your life. This is one of the core-level, structural decisions that lay the foundation for your future.

Let's begin with the first choice and explore how it will affect your life. If you decide you have to keep things from touching the thorn, then that becomes the work of a lifetime. If you want to go for a walk in the woods, you'll have to thin out the branches to make sure you don't brush against them. Since you often roll over and touch the thorn when you sleep, you'll have to find a solution for that as well. Perhaps you could design an apparatus that acts as a protective device. If you really put a lot of energy into it and your solution seemed to work, you would think that you had solved your problem. You'd say, "I can sleep now. And guess what? I got to go on TV to give a testimonial. Anybody who has the thorn problem can get my protective device, and I even get paid royalties."

So now you've got a whole life built around this thorn, and you're proud of it. You keep the woods thinned out, and you wear the apparatus to bed at night. But now you have a new problem—you fell in love. This is a problem because in your situation, it's hard to even hug. Nobody can touch you because they might touch the thorn. So you design another kind of device that allows closeness amongst people without actually touching.

Eventually you decide you want total mobility without having to worry about the thorn anymore. So you make a full-time device that doesn't have to be unstrapped at night or changed over for hugging and other daily activities. But it's heavy. So you put wheels on it, control it with hydraulics, and install collision sensors. It's actually quite an impressive device.

Of course, you had to change the doors in the house so that the protective apparatus could get through. But at least now you can live your life. You can go to work, go to sleep, and get close to people. So you announce to everyone, "I have solved my problem. I am a free being. I can go anywhere I want. I can do anything I want. This thorn used to run my life. Now it doesn't run anything."

The truth is, the thorn completely runs your entire life. It affects all your decisions, including where you go, whom you're comfortable with, and who's comfortable with you. It determines where you're allowed to work, what house you can live in, and what kind of bed you can sleep on at night. When it's all said and done, that thorn is running every aspect of your life.

It turns out that the life of protecting yourself from your problem becomes a perfect reflection of the problem itself. You didn't solve anything. If you don't solve the root cause of the problem, but instead, attempt to protect yourself from the problem, it ends up running your life.

Removing Your Inner Thorn

You end up so psychologically fixated on the problem that you can't see the forest for the trees. You actually feel that because you've minimized the pain of the problem, you've solved the problem. But it is not solved. All you did was devote your life to avoiding it. It is now the center of your universe. It's all there is.

In order to apply the analogy of the thorn to your whole life, we will use loneliness as an example. Let's say you have a very deep sense of inner loneliness. It's so deep that you have trouble sleeping at night, and during the day it makes you very sensitive. You're susceptible to feeling sharp pangs in your heart that cause quite a disturbance. You have trouble staying focused on your job, and you have trouble with everyday interactions. What's more, when you're very lonely it's often painfully difficult to get close to people. You see, loneliness is just like the thorn. It causes pain and disturbance in all aspects of your life. But in the case of the human heart, we have more than one thorn. We have sensitivities about loneliness, about rejection, about our physical appearance, and about our mental prowess. We are walking around with lots of thorns touching right against the most sensitive part of our hearts. At any moment something can touch them and cause pain inside.

You have the same two choices with these inner thorns as you did with the thorn in your arm. Surely it was obvious that you would have been much better off taking out that thorn. There's no reason to spend your life protecting the thorn from getting touched when you can just remove it. Once the thorn is removed, you are truly free of it. The same is true with your inner thorns; they can be removed. But if you choose to keep them without being disturbed by them, you must modify your life to avoid the situations that would stir them up. If you're lonely, you must avoid going to places where couples tend to be. If you're afraid of rejection, you must avoid getting too close to people. If you do this, however, it is for the same reason that you thinned out the woods. You are attempting to adjust your life to make allowance for your thorns. In the earlier example the thorns were outside. Now they are inside.

When you're lonely, you find yourself pondering what to do about your loneliness. What is it that you can say or do in order to not feel so lonely? Notice that you aren't asking how to get rid of the problem; you're asking how to protect yourself from feeling it. You do this either by avoiding situations or by using people, places, and things as protective shields. You're going to end up just like the person with the thorn. The loneliness will run your entire life. You'll marry the person who makes you feel less lonely, and you'll think that's natural and normal. But it's exactly the same as the person who is avoiding the pain of the thorn instead of taking it out. You have not removed the root of loneliness. You have only attempted to protect yourself from feeling it. Should someone die or leave you, the loneliness would again disturb you. The problem will be back the moment the external situation fails to protect you from what's inside.

If you do not remove the thorn, you will end up responsible for both the thorn and everything you pulled around yourself in an attempt to avoid it. Should you be fortunate enough to find someone who manages to diminish the feeling of loneliness, you will then begin worrying about keeping your relationship with this person. You've managed to compound the issue by avoiding the problem. This is exactly the same as using the apparatus to compensate for the thorn; you have to adjust your life accordingly. The minute you allow the core problem to stay, it expands out into multiple problems. It wouldn't dawn on you to just get rid of it. Instead, the only solution you see is to try to avoid feeling it. Now you have no choice but to go out and fix everything that affects it. You have to worry about how you dress and how you talk. You have to worry about what people think of you because that could affect your feeling of loneliness or need for love. If someone is attracted to you, and this eases your feelings of loneliness, you wish you could say, "How do I need to act in order to please you? I can be any way you want. I just don't want to feel these periods of loneliness anymore."

You now have this burden of worrying about the relationship. It creates an experience of underlying tension and discomfort, and it can even affect your sleep at night. The truth is, however, the discomfort you're experiencing isn't actually the feeling of loneliness. It's the never-ending thoughts of "Did I say the right thing? Does she really like me, or am I just kidding myself?" The root problem is now buried under all these shallower issues that are all about avoiding the deeper ones. It all gets very complicated. People end up using their relationships to hide their thorns. If you care for each other, you are expected to adjust your behavior to avoid bumping into each other's soft spots.

This is what people do. They let the fear of their inner thorns affect their behavior. They end up limiting their lives just like someone living with an external thorn. Ultimately, if there is something disturbing inside of you, you have to make a choice. You can compensate for the disturbance by going outside in an attempt to avoid feeling it, or you can simply remove the thorn and not focus your life around it.

Do not doubt your ability to remove the root cause of the disturbance inside of you. It really can go away. You can look deep within yourself, to the core of your being, and decide that you don't want the weakest part of you running your life. You want to be free of this. You want to talk to people because you find them interesting, not because you're lonely. You want to have relationships with people because you genuinely like them, not because you need for them to like you. You want to love because you truly love, not because you need to avoid your inner problems.

How do you free yourself? In the deepest sense, you free yourself by finding yourself. You are not the pain you feel, nor are you the part that periodically stresses out. None of these disturbances have anything to do with you. You are the one who notices these things. Because your consciousness is separate and aware of these things, you can free yourself. To free yourself of your inner thorns, you simply stop playing with them. The more you touch them, the more you irritate them. Because you're always doing something to avoid feeling them, they are not given the chance to naturally work themselves out. If you want, you can simply permit the disturbances to come up, and you can let them go. Since your inner thorns are simply blocked energies from the past, they can be released. The problem is, you either completely avoid situations that would cause them to release, or you push them back down in the name of protecting yourself.

Suppose you're sitting at home watching TV. You're enjoying the program until the two main characters fall in love. Suddenly you feel loneliness, but there's no one around to give you attention. Interestingly, you were fine just a few minutes ago. This example shows that the thorn is always in your heart; it's just not activated until something touches it. You feel the reaction as a hollowness or a dropping sensation in your heart. It feels very uncomfortable. A sense of weakness comes over you, and you begin thinking about other times when you were left alone and of people who have hurt you. Stored energy from the past releases from the heart and generates thoughts. Now, instead of enjoying TV, you're sitting alone caught in a wave of thoughts and emotions.

What can you do to solve this besides eating something, calling somebody, or doing something else that might quiet it down? What you can do is notice that you noticed. You can notice that your consciousness was watching TV, and now it is watching your inner melodrama. The one who sees this is you, the subject. What you are looking at is an object. A feeling of emptiness is an object; it is something you feel. But who feels it? Your way out is to just notice who's noticing. It's really that simple. It is much less complex than the protective apparatus with all its ball bearings, wheels, and hydraulics. All you have to do is notice who it is that feels the loneliness. The one who notices is already free. If you want to be free of these energies, you must allow them to pass through you instead of hiding them inside of you.

Ever since you were a child, you've had energies going on inside. Wake up and realize that you are in there, and you have a sensitive person in there with you. Simply watch that sensitive part of you feel disturbance. See it feel jealousy, need, and fear. These feelings are just part of the nature of a human being. If you pay attention, you will see that they are not you; they are just something you're feeling and experiencing. You are the indwelling being that is aware of all of this. If you maintain your center, you can learn to appreciate and respect even the difficult experiences.

For example, some of the most beautiful poetry and music have come from people who were in turmoil. Great art comes from the depth of one's being. You can experience these very human states without getting lost in them or resisting them. You can notice that you notice and just watch how experiencing loneliness affects you. Does your posture change? Do you breathe slower or faster? What goes on when loneliness is given the space it needs to pass through you? Be an explorer. Witness it, and then it will go. If you don't get absorbed in it, the experience will soon pass and something else will come up. Just enjoy all of it. If you can do this, you will be free, and a world of pure energy will open up within you.

The more you sit in the Self, the more you will begin to feel an energy that you have never experienced before. It comes up from behind, rather than in front where you experience your mind and emotions. When you are no longer absorbed in your melodrama but, instead, sit comfortably deep inside the seat of awareness, you will start to feel this flow of energy coming up from deep within. This flow has been called Shakti. This flow has been called Spirit. This is what you begin to experience if you hang out with the Self instead of hanging out with inner disturbances. You don't have to get rid of loneliness; you just cease to be involved with it. It's just another thing in the universe, like cars, grass, and the stars. It's none of your business. Just let things go. That's what the Self does. Awareness does not fight; awareness releases. Awareness is simply aware while everything in the universe parades before it.

If you sit within the Self, you will experience the strength of your inner being even when your heart feels weak. This is the essence of the path. This is the essence of a spiritual life. Once you learn that it's okay to feel inner disturbances, and that they can no longer disturb your seat of consciousness, you will be free. You will begin to be sustained by the inner energy flow that comes from behind you. When you have tasted the ecstasy of the inner flow, you can walk in this world and the world will never touch you. That's how you become a free being— you transcend.

CHAPTER 10

stealing freedom
for your soul

The prerequisite to true freedom is to decide that you do not want to suffer anymore. You must decide that you want to enjoy your life and that there is no reason for stress, inner pain, or fear. Every day we bear a burden that we should not be bearing. We fear that we are not good enough or that we will fail. We experience insecurity, anxiety, and self-consciousness. We fear that people will turn on us, take advantage of us, or stop loving us. All of these things burden us tremendously. As we try to have open and loving relationships, and as we try to succeed and express ourselves, there is an inner weight that we carry. This weight is the fear of experiencing pain, anguish, or sorrow. Every day we are either feeling it, or we are protecting ourselves from feeling it. It is such a core influence that we don't even realize how prevalent it is.

When Buddha said that all of life is suffering, this is what he was referring to. People do not understand how much they are suffering because they have never experienced what it is like to not suffer. To put this into perspective, imagine what it would be like if neither you, nor anyone you know, has ever been healthy. Everyone has always had major ailments so acute that they can hardly get out of bed. In this world, nothing gets done that can't be done near the bedside. If that were the case, then people wouldn't know anything different. They would have to use all their energy just to drag their bodies along, and there would be no concept or understanding of health and vitality.

That is exactly what is going on with the mental and emotional energies that make up your psyche. Your inner sensitivities expose you to a minute-to-minute, constant situation in which you are suffering to one degree or another. You are either trying to stop suffering, controlling your environment to avoid suffering, or worrying about suffering in the future. This state of affairs is so prevalent that you don't see it, just as a fish doesn't see the water.

You only notice that you're suffering when it gets worse than usual. You admit you have a problem when it gets so bad that it actually begins to affect your everyday behavior. But in truth, you are having constant issues with your psyche during your normal daily life. To truly see this, compare your relationship with your mind to your relationship with your body. Under normal, healthy situations, you are not thinking about your body. You just go about your business walking, driving, working, and playing without focusing on it. You only think about your body when there is a problem. In contrast, you think about your psychological well-being all the time. People are constantly thinking things like, "What if I get put on the spot? What should I say? I get so nervous if I'm not prepared." That is suffering. That constant, anxious inner talk is a form of suffering: "Can I really trust him? What if I expose myself and I get taken advantage of? I don't ever want to go through that again." That is the pain of having to think about yourself all the time.

Why do we have to think about ourselves all the time? Why are so many thoughts about I, me, and mine? Look how often you think about how you're doing, whether you like things or not, and how to rearrange the world to please yourself. You think like this because you're not okay inside, and you're constantly trying to make yourself feel better. If your body had not been okay for a very long time, you'd find yourself constantly thinking about how to protect it and how to make it feel better. This is exactly what is going on with your psyche. The only reason that you think about your psychological well-being so much is because it has not been okay for a very long time. It's actually quite fragile in there. Just about anything can upset the psyche.

To end suffering, you must first realize that your psyche is not okay. You must then acknowledge that it does not have to be that way. It can be healthy. It is truly a gift just to realize that you don't have to put up with, or protect, your psyche. You don't have to constantly be mulling over what you said or what this person thinks of you. What kind of life are you going to have if you worry about these things all the time? Inner sensitivity is a symptom of non-well-being. It's the same as when the body sends pain or displays other symptoms when it's not well. Pain is not bad; it's how the body talks to you. When you overeat, you get a stomachache. When you do something that puts too much stress on your arm, it starts to hurt. The body is communicating through its universal language: pain. Your psyche is communicating through its universal language: fear. Self-consciousness, jealousy, insecurity, anxiety—they are all fear.

If you mistreat an animal, it becomes afraid. This is what has happened to your psyche. You have mistreated it by giving it a responsibility that is incomprehensible. Just stop for a moment and see what you have given your mind to do. You said to your mind, "I want everyone to like me. I don't want anyone to speak badly of me. I want everything I say and do to be acceptable and pleasing to everyone. I don't want anyone to hurt me. I don't want anything to happen that I don't like. And I want everything to happen that I do like." Then you said, "Now, mind, figure out how to make every one of these things a reality, even if you have to think about it day and night." And of course your mind said, "I'm on the job. I will work on it constantly."

Can you imagine somebody trying to do that? The mind has to try to make it so that everything you say is said the right way, taken the right way, and has the right effect on everybody. It has to make sure that everything you do is interpreted and seen the right way, and that nobody does anything that hurts you. It has to make sure that you get everything you want, and that you don't ever get what you don't want. The mind is constantly trying to give you advice about how to make it all okay. That is why the mind is so active; you gave it an impossible task to do. It's equivalent to expecting your body to lift trees and scale mountains in a single jump. Your body would get sick if you kept trying to make it do things it was incapable of doing. This is what has broken the psyche. The signs of the body breaking are pain and weakness. The signs of the psyche breaking are underlying fear and incessant neurotic thought.

At some point, you have to wake up and acknowledge that you have a problem inside. Just watch and you'll see that your mind is constantly telling you what to do. It tells you to go here, but not there, and to say this, but not that. It tells you what to wear and what not to wear. It has never stopped. Wasn't it that way in high school? Wasn't it that way in junior high and elementary school? Hasn't it always been that way? This act of constantly worrying about yourself is a form of suffering. But how do you fix this? How do you get it to stop?

Most people try to fix their inner problems by getting better at the same external games they have always played. If we take a snapshot of our inner problems, we will see that each person has what we'll call the "problem of the day." This is the thing that is bothering them the most at any given moment. When the current problem isn't bothering them, then the next one pops up, and when that one isn't bothering them, the next one pops up. That is what your thoughts are about. Your thoughts tend to focus on what is bothering you today. Your thoughts are about the problem, why it is bothering you, and what you can do about it. If you don't do something about this, it will go on for the rest of your life.

What you'll see is that your mind is always telling you that you have to change something outside in order to solve your inner problems. But if you are wise, you won't play this game. You'll realize that the advice your mind is giving you is psychologically damaged advice. Your mind's thoughts are disturbed by its fears. Of all the advice in the world that you do not want to listen to, it is the advice of a disturbed mind. Your mind actually misleads you. Suppose it tells you, "If I could just get that promotion, then I'd be fine. I'd feel good about myself, and I could get my life back together." Have you

141

found that to be true? After you get the promotion, does that end all your insecurities and leave you financially satisfied for the rest of your life? Of course not. All that happens is that the next problem comes to the surface.

Once you see this, you realize the mind has a serious underlying problem. And what it's doing is making up external situations that might make things more comfortable. But the external situations are not the cause of the inner problem. They are merely an attempt to solve the problem. For example, if you feel loneliness and insufficiency within your heart, it's not because you haven't found a special relationship. That did not cause the problem. That relationship is your attempt to solve the problem. All you're doing is trying to see if a relationship will appease your inner disturbance. If it doesn't, you'll try something else.

The fact is, however, external changes are not going to solve your problem because they don't address the root of your problem. The root problem is that you don't feel whole and complete within yourself. If you don't identify the root properly, you will seek someone or something to cover it up. You will hide behind finances, people, fame, and adoration. If you try to find the perfect person to love and adore you, and you manage to succeed, then you have actually failed. You did not solve your problem. All you did was involve that person in your problem.

That is why people have so much trouble with relationships. You began with a problem inside yourself, and you tried to solve it by getting involved with somebody else. That relationship will have problems because your problems are what caused the relationship. It is all so easy to see once you step back and dare to look at it honestly.

Now that we've seen what failure looks like, let's define success. Success regarding your psyche is comparable to health regarding your physical body. Success means you never have to think about your psyche again. A naturally healthy body is one that just does what it's supposed to do while you're going about your business. You never have to think about it. Likewise, you should never have to figure out how to be okay, or how not to be scared, or how to feel loved. You should not have to devote your life to your psyche.

Imagine what fun life would be if you didn't have those neurotic, personal thoughts going on within you. You could enjoy things, and you could actually get to know people instead of needing them. You could just live and experience your life, instead of trying to use life to fix what's wrong inside of you. You are capable of achieving that state. It's never too late.

Your current relationship with your psyche is like an addiction. It is constantly making demands of you, and you have devoted your life to serving these demands.

If you want to be free, you have to learn to treat it like any other addiction. For example, drug addicts are capable of stopping their drug use, going through withdrawals, and never doing drugs again. Maybe it isn't easy, but they are capable. The same thing is true of the addiction to the psyche. You are capable of ceasing the absurdity of listening to the perpetual problems of your psyche. You can put an end to it. You can wake up in the morning, look forward to the day, and not worry about what will happen. Your daily life can be like a vacation. Work can be fun; family can be fun; you can just enjoy all of it. That does not mean you don't do your best; you just have fun doing your best. Then, at night when you go to sleep, you let it all go. You just live your life without getting uptight and worrying about it. You actually live life instead of fearing or fighting it.

You can live a life completely free from the fears of the psyche. You just have to know how to do it. Let's take smoking as an example. It is not hard to understand how to stop smoking. The key word is "stop." It really doesn't matter what patches you use; when it is all said and done, you simply must stop. The way you stop smoking is to stop putting cigarettes in your mouth. All the other techniques are just ways that you think will help. But the bottom line is, all you have to do is stop putting cigarettes in your mouth. If you do this, it's guaranteed that you will stop smoking.

You use the same technique to get out of your psychological mess. You just stop telling your mind that its job is to fix your personal problems. This job has broken the mind and disturbed the entire psyche. It has created fear, anxiety, and neurosis. Your mind has very little control over this world. It is neither omniscient nor omnipotent. It cannot control the weather and other natural forces. Nor can it control all people, places, and things around you. You have given your mind an impossible task by asking it to manipulate the world in order to fix your personal inner problems. If you want to achieve a healthy state of being, stop asking your mind to do this. Just relieve your mind of the job of making sure that everyone and everything will be the way you need them to be so that you can feel better inside. Your mind is not qualified for that job. Fire it, and let go of your inner problems instead.

You can have a different relationship with your mind. Whenever it starts up telling you what you should or shouldn't do in order to get the world to match your preconceived concepts, don't listen. It's just like when you try to stop smoking. Regardless of what your mind says, you don't pick up a cigarette and put it in your mouth. It doesn't matter if it is just after dinner. It doesn't matter if you get anxious and you feel the need. It doesn't matter what the reason is—your hand simply does not touch cigarettes anymore. Likewise, when your mind starts telling you what you have to do to make everything inside okay, don't buy into what it's telling you. The truth is, everything will be okay as soon as you are okay with everything. And that's the only time everything will be okay.

All you have to do is stop expecting the mind to fix what's wrong inside of you. That is the core, the root of it all. Your mind is not the guilty party. In fact, your mind is innocent. The mind is simply a computer, a tool. It can be used to ponder great thoughts, solve scientific problems, and serve humanity. But you, in your lost state, told it to spend its time conjuring up outer solutions for your very personal inner problems. You are the one who is trying to use the analytical mind to protect yourself from the natural unfolding of life.

By watching your mind, you will notice that it is engaged in the process of trying to make everything okay. Consciously remember that this is not what you want to do, and then gently disengage. Do not fight it. Do not ever fight your mind. You will never win. It will either beat you now, or you will suppress it and it will come back and beat you later. Instead of fighting the mind, just don't participate in it. When you see the mind

152

telling you how to fix the world and everyone in it in order to suit yourself, just don't listen.

The key is to be quiet. It's not that your mind has to be quiet. You be quiet. You, the one inside watching the neurotic mind, just relax. You will then naturally fall behind the mind because you have always been there. You are not the thinking mind; you are aware of the thinking mind. You are the consciousness that is behind the mind and is aware of the thoughts. The minute you stop putting your whole heart and soul into the mind as if it were your savior and protector, you will find yourself behind the mind watching it. That's how you know about your thoughts: you are in there watching them. Eventually, you will be able to just sit in there quietly, and consciously watch the mind.

Once you reach that state, your problems with the mind are over. When you pull back behind the mind, you, the awareness, are not involved in the process of thinking. Thinking is something you watch the mind do. You are just in there, aware that you are aware. You are the indwelling being, the consciousness. It is not something that you have to think about; you are it. You can watch the mind being neurotic and not get involved. That is all you have to do to unplug the disturbed mind. The mind runs because you are giving it the power of your attention. Withdraw your attention, and the thinking mind falls away.

Begin with the little things. For example, somebody says something to you that you don't like, or worse yet, doesn't acknowledge you at all. You are walking along and you see a friend. You say hello to them but they just keep walking by. You don't know if they didn't hear you or if they actually ignored you. You aren't sure if they're mad at you or what's going on. Your mind starts going a mile a minute. Good time for a reality check! There are billions of people on this planet, and one of them didn't say hello to you. Are you saying that you can't handle that? Is that reasonable?

Use these little things that happen in daily life to free yourself. In the above example, you simply choose not to get involved in the psyche. Does that mean that you stop your mind from going around in circles trying to figure out what's going on? No. It simply means that you are ready, willing, and able to watch your mind create its little melodrama. Watch all of its noise about how hurt you are, and how could anybody do that. Watch the mind try to figure out what to do about it. Just marvel at the fact that all of this is going on inside simply because someone didn't say hello to you. It's truly unbelievable. Just watch the mind talk, and keep relaxing and releasing. Fall behind the noise.

Just keep doing this with all those little things that come up each day. It is a very private thing you do inside yourself. You will soon see that your mind is constantly driving you crazy over nothing. If you don't want to be like that, then stop putting energy into your psyche. That is all there is to it. If you follow this path, the only action you ever take is to relax and release. When you start to see this stuff going on inside, you just relax your shoulders, relax your heart, and fall back behind it. Do not touch it. Do not get involved in it. And do not try to stop it. Simply be aware that you are seeing it. That's how you get out. You just let it go.

Begin this journey to freedom by regularly reminding yourself to watch the psyche. This will keep you from getting lost in it. Because the addiction to the personal mind is a major one, you must set up a method to remind yourself to watch. There are some very simple awareness practices that only take a second to do, yet will help you stay centered behind the mind. Every time you get into your car, as you're settling into the seat, just stop. Take a moment to remember that you're spinning on a planet in the middle of empty space. Then remind yourself that you're not going to get involved in your own melodrama. In other words, let go of what is going on right then, and remind yourself that you don't want to play the mind game. Then, before you get out of your car, do the same thing. And if you really want to stay centered, you can also do this before you pick up the phone or open a door. You don't have to change anything. Just be there, noticing that you notice. It's like taking inventory. Just check out what's going on—heart, mind, shoulders, etc. Set up trigger points in everyday life that help you remember who you are and what's going on inside.

These practices create moments of centered consciousness. Eventually, you will have persistently centered consciousness. Persistently centered consciousness is the seat of Self. In this state, you are always conscious of being conscious. There is never a time when you're not totally aware. There is no effort. There is no doing anything. You're just there, aware that thoughts and emotions are being created around you, while the world unfolds before your senses.

Ultimately, every change in your energy flow, whether it's agitation of the mind or shifts in the heart, will be what reminds you that you are back there noticing. Now what used to hold you down becomes what wakes you up. But first you have to get quiet enough so that it's not so reactive in there. These trigger points will help remind you to remain centered. Eventually it will become quiet enough so that you can simply watch the heart begin to react, and let go before the mind starts. At some point in the journey it all becomes heart, not mind. You will see that the mind follows the heart. The heart reacts way before the mind starts talking. When you are conscious, the shifts of energy in your heart cause you to instantaneously be aware that you are back there noticing. The mind doesn't even get a chance to start up because you let go at the heart level.

Now you are on your way. The very thing that was holding you in is now helping you out. You have to use all energies to your advantage. This path of letting go allows you to free your energies so that you can free yourself. Right in the midst of your daily life, by untethering yourself from the bondage of your psyche, you actually have the ability to steal freedom for your soul. This freedom is so great it has been given a special name—liberation.

CHAPTER 11

pain, the price of freedom

One of the essential requirements for true spiritual growth and deep personal transformation is coming to peace with pain. No expansion or evolution can take place without change, and periods of change are not always comfortable. Change involves challenging what is familiar to us and daring to question our traditional needs for safety, comfort, and control. This is often perceived as a painful experience.

Becoming familiar with this pain is part of your growth. Even though you may not actually like the feelings of inner disturbance, you must be able to sit quietly inside and face them if you want to see where they come from. Once you can face your disturbances, you will realize that there is a layer of pain seated deep in the core of your heart. This pain is so uncomfortable, so challenging, and so destructive to the individual self, that your entire life is spent avoiding it. Your entire personality is built upon ways of being, thinking, acting, and believing that were developed to avoid this pain.

Since avoiding the pain prohibits you from exploring the part of your being that is beyond that layer, real growth takes place when you finally decide to deal with the pain. Because the pain is at the core of the heart, it radiates out and affects everything you do. But this pain is not the physical pain that you receive as messages from your body. Physical pain is only there when something is physiologically wrong. Inner pain is always there, underneath, hidden by the layers of our thoughts and emotions. We feel it most when our hearts go into turmoil, like when the world does not meet our expectations. This is an inner, psychological pain.

The psyche is built upon avoiding this pain, and as a result, it has fear of pain as its foundation. That is what caused the psyche to be. To understand this, notice that if the feeling of rejection is a major problem for you, you will fear experiences that cause rejection. That fear will become part of your psyche. Even though the actual events causing rejection are infrequent, you will have to deal with the fear of rejection all the time. That is how we create a pain that is always there. If you are doing something to avoid pain, then pain is running your life. All of your thoughts and feelings will be affected by your fears.

You will come to see that any behavior pattern based upon the avoidance of pain becomes a doorway to the pain itself. If you are afraid of being rejected by someone and you approach that person with the intention of winning their acceptance, you are skating on thin ice. All they have to do is look at you sideways or say the wrong thing, and you will feel the pain of rejection. The bottom line is that since you approached them in the name of rejection, you're going to be dancing on the edge of rejection throughout the interaction. One way or another, the feelings you experience will work their way back to the motive behind your actions. The avoidance of pain is what your actions are linked to, and you will feel that link in your heart.

The heart is where pain comes from. And this is why you feel so many disturbances as you go through the day. You have this core of pain deep in your heart. Your personality traits and behavior patterns are all about avoiding this pain. You avoid it by keeping your weight a certain way, wearing certain clothes, talking a certain way, and choosing a certain hairstyle. Everything you do is about the avoidance of this pain. If you want to validate this, just see what happens if someone mentions your weight or criticizes your clothes: you feel pain. Every time you do something in the name of avoiding pain, that something becomes a link that holds the potential for the pain you're avoiding.

If you do not want to deal with the pain at its core, then what you do to avoid it had better work. If you are hiding yourself in a busy social life, then anything anyone does that challenges your self-esteem, such as not inviting you to an event, will cause you to feel the pain. Let's say you call a friend to go see a movie, and they say they're busy. Some people feel hurt by that. You will feel pain if the reason you called them was the avoidance of pain. Let's say you go outside and you call your dog, "Hey, Spot, come here!" and he doesn't come. If the reason you called Spot was to feed him, you'd just put the bowl down and let him eat when he wants. But if you called Spot because you had a hard day, and Spot didn't come, you would feel pain. "Even the dog doesn't like me." Why would there be heartfelt pain in the dog not coming? Why would there be pain in a friend saying they are going someplace else and they can't go to the movie today? How does that generate pain? It is because deep inside there is pain that you have not processed. Your attempt to avoid this pain has created layer upon layer of sensitivities that are all linked to the hidden pain.

Let's take a moment to see how these layers build up. In order to avoid the pain of rejection, you work hard to maintain friendships. Since you've seen that it is possible to get rejected, even by friends, you are going to work harder and harder to avoid it. To succeed, you have to be sure everything you do is acceptable to others. This determines how you dress and how you act. Notice, you're no longer focused directly on rejection. Now it's about your clothes, how you walk, or what you drive. You've gone another layer further away from the core pain. If somebody comes up to you and says, "Wow, I thought you could afford a nicer car than that!" you feel a disturbing reaction. How could that cause pain? What's the big deal if somebody says something about your car? You have to ask yourself what it is that reacted in your heart. What is that feeling? Why is that happening? People don't normally ask why; they just try to keep it from happening.

You must go deeper than that and look at the dynamics of the layers that have been created. At the core there is the pain. Then, in order to avoid the pain, you try to stay busy with friends and hide in their acceptance. That is the first layer out. Then, in order to assure your acceptance, you try to present yourself a certain way so that you can win friends and influence people. That is another layer out. Each layer is attached to the original pain. This is why simple, everyday interactions can affect you so much. If the core pain was not the motivation behind proving yourself each day, what people say would not affect you. But since avoiding the core pain is why you're trying to prove yourself, you end up bringing the potential for pain into everything that happens. You end up so sensitive that you are unable to live in this world without getting hurt. You cannot even interact with people or do other normal daily activities without events affecting your heart. If you watch carefully, you will see that even simple interactions often cause some degree of pain, insecurity, or general disturbance.

Pain, the Price of Freedom

To get some distance from this, you first need to get some perspective. Walk outside on a clear night and just look up into the sky. You are sitting on a planet spinning around in the middle of absolutely nowhere. Though you can only see a few thousand stars, there are hundreds of billions of stars in our Milky Way Galaxy alone. In fact, it is estimated that there are over a trillion stars in the Spiral Galaxy. And that galaxy would look like one star to us, if we could even see it. You're just standing on one little ball of dirt and spinning around one of the stars. From that perspective, do you really care what people think about your clothes or your car? Do you really need to feel embarrassed if you forget someone's name? How can you let these meaningless things cause pain? If you want out, if you want a decent life, you had better not devote your life to avoiding psychological pain. You had better not spend your life worrying about whether people like you or whether your car impresses people. What kind of life is that? It is a life of pain. You may not think that you feel pain that often, but you really do. To spend your life avoiding pain means it's always right behind you. At any point you could slip and say the wrong thing. At any point anything can happen. So you end up devoting your life to the avoidance of pain.

Once you look inside yourself and start to own this, you will see that you are back to the same two foundational choices. One choice is to leave the pain inside and continue to struggle with the outside. The other choice is to decide that you don't want to spend your entire life avoiding the inner pain; you'd rather get rid of it. Few people ever dare to turn the process inside like this. Most people don't even realize that they are running around with pockets of pain inside that need to be worked out. Do you really want to carry that inside and have to manipulate the world to avoid feeling it? What would your life be like if it wasn't run by that pain? You would be free. You could walk around this world completely free, just having fun, just being comfortable with whatever happens. You can actually live a life full of interesting experiences and just enjoy these experiences whatever they are. In essence, you can simply live your life and experience what it's like to be on a planet that is spinning around in the middle of nowhere, until you die.

To live at this level of freedom, you must learn not to be afraid of inner pain and disturbance. As long as you are afraid of the pain, you will try to protect yourself from it. The fear will make you do that. If you want to be free, simply view inner pain as a temporary shift in your energy flow. There is no reason to fear this experience. You must not be afraid of rejection, or of how you would feel if you got sick, or if someone died, or if something else went wrong. You cannot spend your life avoiding things that are not actually happening, or everything will become negative. All you will end up seeing is how much can potentially go wrong. Do you have any idea how many things can cause inner pain and disturbance? Probably more than there are stars in the sky. If you want to grow and be free to explore life, you cannot spend your life avoiding the myriad things that might hurt your heart or mind.

You must look inside yourself and determine that from now on pain is not a problem. It is just a thing in the universe. Somebody can say something to you that can cause your heart to react and catch fire, but then it passes. It's a temporary experience. Most people can hardly imagine what it would be like to be at peace with inner disturbance. But if you do not learn to be comfortable with it, you will devote your life to avoiding it. If you feel insecurity, it's just a feeling. You can handle a feeling. If you feel embarrassed, it's just a feeling. It's just a part of creation. If you feel jealousy and your heart burns, just look at it objectively, like you would a mild bruise. It's a thing in the universe that is passing through your system. Laugh at it, have fun with it, but don't be afraid of it. It cannot touch you unless you touch it.

Let's explore this by first looking at a basic human tendency. When something painful touches your body, you tend to pull away instinctively. You even do this with unpleasant smells and tastes. The fact is, your psyche does the same thing. If something disturbing touches it, its tendency is to withdraw, to pull back, and to protect itself. It does this with insecurity, jealousy, and any of the other vibrations we've been discussing. In essence, you "close," which is simply an attempt to put a shield around your inner energy. You can feel the effects of this as the sensation of contracting within your heart. Somebody says something displeasing, and you feel some disturbance in your heart. Then your mind starts talking: "I don't have to put up with this. I'll just walk away and never talk to them again. They'll be sorry." Your heart is attempting to pull back from what it's experiencing and protect itself so that it doesn't have to experience that feeling again. You do this because you can't handle the pain you're feeling. As long as you can't handle the pain, you will react by closing in order to protect yourself. Once you close, your mind will build an entire psychological structure around your closed energy. Your thoughts will try to rationalize why you're right, why the other person's wrong, and what you should do about it.

If you buy into this, it will become a part of you. For years the pain will remain inside and actually become one of the building blocks of your entire life. It will shape your future reactions, thoughts, and preferences. When you deal with a situation by resisting the pain it causes, you will have to adjust your behavior and thoughts in order to protect yourself. You will have to do this so that nothing aggravates what you have held inside about the incident. You will end up building an entire protection structure around the closure. If you have the clarity to watch this happen, and understand the long-term consequences, you will want to be free of this trap. You will never be free, however, until you get to the point where you are willing to release the initial pain instead of avoiding it. You must learn to transcend the tendency to avoid the pain.

Wise beings do not want to remain a slave to the fear of pain. They permit the world to be what it is instead of being afraid of it. They wholeheartedly participate in life, but not for the purpose of using life to avoid themselves. If life does something that causes a disturbance inside of you, instead of pulling away, let it pass through you like the wind. After all, things happen every day that cause inner disturbance. At any moment you can feel frustration, anger, fear, jealousy, insecurity, or embarrassment. If you watch, you will see that the heart is trying to push it all away. If you want to be free, you have to learn to stop fighting these human feelings.

When you feel pain, simply view it as energy. Just start seeing these inner experiences as energy passing through your heart and before the eye of your consciousness. Then relax. Do the opposite of contracting and closing. Relax and release. Relax your heart until you are actually face-to-face with the exact place where it hurts. Stay open and receptive so you can be present right where the tension is. You must be willing to be present right at the place of the tightness and pain, and then relax and go even deeper. This is very deep growth and transformation. But you will not want to do this. You will feel tremendous resistance to doing this, and that's what makes it so powerful. As you relax and feel the resistance, the heart will want to pull away, to close, to protect, and to defend itself. Keep relaxing. Relax your shoulders and relax your heart. Let go and give room for the pain to pass through you. It's just energy. Just see it as energy and let it go.

If you close around the pain and stop it from passing through, it will stay in you. That is why our natural tendency to resist is so counterproductive. If you don't want the pain, why do you close around it and keep it? Do you actually think that if you resist, it will go away? It's not true. If you release and let the energy pass through, then it will go away. If you relax when the pain comes up inside your heart, and actually dare to face it, it will pass. Every single time you relax and release, a piece of the pain leaves forever. Yet every time you resist and close, you are building up the pain inside. It's like damming up a stream. You are then forced to use the psyche to create a layer of distance between you who experiences the pain and the pain itself. That is what all the noise is inside your mind: an attempt to avoid the stored pain.

If you want to be free, you must first accept that there is pain in your heart. You have stored it there. And you've done everything you can think of to keep it there, deep inside, so that you never have to feel it. There is also tremendous joy, beauty, love, and peace within you. But they are on the other side of the pain. On the other side of the pain is ecstasy. On the other side is freedom. Your true greatness hides on the other side of that layer of pain. You must be willing to accept pain in order to pass through to the other side. Just accept that it is in there and that you are going to feel it. Accept that if you relax, it will have its moment before your awareness, and then it will pass. It always does.

Sometimes you will notice that it feels hot inside as pain passes. In fact, as you relax into the energy of the pain, you may feel tremendous heat in your heart. That is the pain being purified from your heart. Learn to enjoy that burning. It is called the fire of yoga. It does not seem enjoyable, but you will learn to enjoy it because it is freeing you. In truth, pain is the price of freedom. And the moment you are willing to pay that price, you will no longer be afraid. The moment you are not afraid of the pain, you'll be able to face all of life's situations without fear.

Sometimes you will go through deep experiences that bring up intense pain inside of you. If it is in there, it is going to come up. If you have any wisdom, you will leave it alone and not try to change your life to avoid it. You will just relax and give it the space it needs to release and burn through you. You do not want this stuff inside your heart. To feel great love and freedom, to find the presence of God within you, all of this stored pain must go. It is in this inner work that spirituality becomes a reality. Spiritual growth exists in that moment when you are consciously willing to pay the price of freedom. You must be willing at all times, in all circumstances, to remain conscious in the face of pain and to work with your heart by relaxing and remaining open.

Remember, if you close around something, you will be psychologically sensitive about that subject for the rest of your life. Because you stored it inside of you, you will be afraid that it will happen again. But if you relax instead of closing, it will work its way through you. If you stay open, the blocked energy inside of you will release naturally, and you will not take on any more.

This is the core of spiritual work. When you are comfortable with pain passing through you, you will be free. This world will never be able to bother you again

Pain, the Price of Freedom

because the worst the world can do is to hit the pain stored within you. If you do not care, if you are no longer afraid of yourself, you are free. You will then be able to walk through this world more vibrant and alive than ever before. You will feel everything at a deeper level. You will begin to have truly beautiful experiences rise up within you. Eventually you will understand that there is an ocean of love behind all of this fear and pain. That force will sustain you by feeding your heart from deep within. Over time, you will form an intensely personal relationship with this beautiful inner force. It will replace the relationship you currently have with inner pain and disturbance. Now peace and love will run your life. When you pass beyond the layer of pain, you will finally be free from the binds of the psyche.

PART IV

going beyond

CHAPTER 12

taking down
the walls

At some point in your growth, it starts to become quieter inside. This happens quite naturally as you take a deeper seat within yourself. You then come to realize that though you have always been in there, you have been completely overwhelmed by the constant barrage of thoughts, emotions, and sensory inputs that draw on your consciousness. As you see this, it begins to dawn on you that you might actually be able to go beyond all these disturbances. The more you sit in the seat of witness consciousness, the more you realize that since you are completely independent of what you are watching, there must be a way to break free of the magical hold that the psyche has on your awareness. There must be a way out.

This inner breakthrough to complete freedom is traditionally depicted by the overused and generally misunderstood term: "enlightenment." The problem is that our views of enlightenment are either based upon our personal experiences or upon our limited conceptual understanding. Since most people have never had experiences in this realm, the state of enlightenment is either scoffed at completely or viewed as the ultimate mystical state accessible to almost no one. It's safe to say that the only thing most people know for sure about enlightenment is that they are not there.

However, with the understanding that thoughts, emotions, and sensory objects are simply passing before your consciousness, it becomes reasonable to question whether your sense of awareness need be limited to this experience. What if consciousness were to remove its focus from your personal set of thoughts, your personal set of emotions, and your limited sensory input? Would you become untethered from the bonds of the personal self and be set free to explore beyond? And how, exactly, did consciousness become bound to the personal self to begin with? The problem with even attempting to consider these questions is that they call for a discussion of what exists beyond the confines of the mind. Obviously, that discussion is very difficult to have from within the mental structure we are so accustomed to using. For this reason, we will begin exploring the untethered state through the use of an allegory. Much like Plato used dialogue to tell his "Allegory of the Cave" in 360 BC, we will use a short story to tell our allegory of a very special house.

Imagine that you found yourself in the midst of an open field where the sun was always shining. It was a beautiful place of great light and great openness. It was so beautiful that you decided you wanted to live there. So you bought the land, and right in the middle of the enormous field, you began personally designing and building the house of your dreams. You put down a solid foundation because you wanted the house to be very strong and to last a long time. You built the house out of concrete blocks so that you wouldn't have any problems with decaying or leaking. To make the house ecologically sound, you decided to put in very few windows and to build a roof with lots of overhang. After you put in the windows, and the house was complete, you realized that a lot of heat still came in. So you installed high-quality protective shutters that not only reflected sunlight and heat back to the outside, but also could be locked down for security purposes. It was a very large house that could store enough supplies to allow for complete self-sufficiency. You even built separate quarters for a quiet acquaintance who would keep the house clean and leave you to be in solitude. And solitude it would be, since your romantic quest included a commitment to no phones, radios, televisions, or Internet connections.

Your house was finally finished, and you were very excited to be living out there. You loved the openness of the field and all the light and beauty of nature. But most of all, you were enamored with the house. You had put your heart and soul into every aspect of the design, and it showed—it was truly "you." In fact, over time, between your infatuation with the house and your growing discomfort with all the strange sights and sounds outside, you started spending more time indoors. It was then that you realized that with the shutters and doors fully locked down, the house actually began to feel like a fortress. And this was just fine with you. Being a city person, it was pretty scary living so far out of touch in total isolation. But you were committed to making it on your own.

So you gradually became accustomed to living safely within the confines of the house. You happily went about your business of reading and writing as you had always longed to do. It was actually quite comfortable in there since it was fully climate controlled, and you had been wise enough to install a modern full-spectrum lighting system. Ironically, you found your house so comfortable, enjoyable, and safe that you stopped thinking about the outside altogether. After all, the inside was familiar, predictable, and within the realm of your control. The outside was unknown, unpredictable, and completely out of your control. Your sense of inner sanctum was supported by the fact that when the shutters and blinds were locked in place they blended like paintings on the walls, and you never even considered risking going outside to unlock them. They were so well made that when the lights were turned off it was absolutely pitch black, day or night. But since you were accustomed to never turning off the lights, you didn't notice this until they started burning out. It was only then that you realized your predicament: no one had left you replacement bulbs compatible with the new system. This meant that once the final light failed, you were left to find your way around the house in absolute darkness.

From that point forward, the only light you had came from the few candles you kept for emergencies. But there were very few of these, so you conserved them well. Being a person who loved light, this was very difficult for you. Yet it was not difficult enough to force you to overcome the fears you had developed about leaving the safety of your house. Eventually, the stress of living in this darkness took its toll on your health, both physically and mentally. With time, the very memory of the beautiful sunlit field began to fade from your mind, never to return again.

You became very concerned about keeping the house lit. The only light you knew about was the light you created in the darkness with your precious candles. It became pretty lonely in there. You were cut off from everything, and the only comfort you felt was the sense of protection your house afforded you. You were no longer aware of exactly what you were so afraid of; you were just aware of always being scared and uncomfortable. It was all you could do just to try to hold yourself together. You even stopped reading and writing because of the lack of light. It was dark, and you too were falling into darkness.

Taking Down the Walls

Then one day, the housekeeper, who shared your overwhelming need to stay in the safety of the house, called you down to the storage cellar. You were amazed by what you saw. A full supply of emergency flashlights had been found that could be powered simply by shaking them. Your housekeeper had already set some up, and the cellar was fully radiant. This was a true turning point in your life.

You set about your business of trying to create light, beauty, and happiness within the confines of your house. You decorated each room and worked together to keep the light shining brightly until you went to sleep. You started reading and writing again, and it turned out that your housemate loved reading your writings. In fact, it was not just the artificial lights that were lighting the house. The ember of love had begun to glow in both of your hearts. Imagine the light you could create together instead of apart. You began spending all of your time with each other, and you even staged a marriage ceremony. It was so beautiful as you vowed to take care of each other and bring love and light into your home. Compared to the darkness in which you had been living, this was heaven.

One day you came across a book in your library. It interested you because it talked about the natural, radiant light that exists "outside." It even spoke of bathing in that light. But it was talking about more light than you could ever imagine, without anyone having to do anything to create it. This was confusing to you. After all, the only light you knew about was the artificial light from candles and flashlights. How could you make that much light and keep it going? You didn't have a clue what this book was talking about because you could only view things in relation to the way you were living. You were living inside the house, and therefore you were living inside of darkness. All the light that you could experience was limited to what you could create within the house. You had lived there for so long that all your hopes, dreams, philosophies, and beliefs were founded upon being inside that dark house. Your whole world was about keeping together the life you had managed to build for yourself within the confines of the house.

When you continued reading this seemingly mystical book, it spoke of what it was like to actually walk around in this natural light. It seemed to be describing a self-luminous, omnipresent light that shines everywhere all at once. It was a light that falls on everything constantly and evenly. Though you had no frame of reference for understanding this, it touched something deep inside of you. The book then discussed actually going outside, that is, going beyond the walls of the world you have created for yourself. In fact, it said that while you are attached and enamored with the world you created to avoid darkness, you will never know the abundance of natural light that is beyond the confines of your house. How will you ever go outside when you are so dependent upon what you have built inside?

The analogy of life inside this house is a perfect fit for our predicament. Our consciousness, our awareness of being, is living deep inside of us in an artificially sealed off area that is absolute. It has four walls, a floor, and a roof. It is so solid that not one ray of natural light comes in. The only light we get is what we manage to create for ourselves. If we don't create good situations for ourselves, there is darkness. So we are very busy decorating daily. We do this by trying to bring things in there with us—hoping to create at least a little light, in the house of our own making, where we have sealed ourselves off.

That is the visual: you are inside a house, totally sealed off from natural light, and the house is sitting in the middle of an open field full of brilliant light. But what is your house made of? What are your walls made of? How can they seal off all that light and keep you locked inside? Your house is made of your thoughts and emotions. The walls are made of your psyche. That's what that house is. It is all your past experiences; all your thoughts and emotions; all the concepts, views, opinions, beliefs, hopes, and dreams that you have collected around yourself. You hold them in place on all sides, including above and below you. You have pulled together in your mind a specific set of thoughts and emotions, and then you have woven them together into a conceptual world in which you live. This mental structure completely blocks you from whatever natural light is on the outside of its walls. You have walls of thoughts thick enough, and closed enough, to where nothing but darkness is inside that structure. You are so entranced into paying attention to your thoughts and emotions that you never go beyond the borders they create.

If you want to see how restrictive your walls are, just start walking toward them. Let's say you have an emotional fear of heights. When you were young you fell off a ladder, and the impression stayed with you. That is one of your walls. If you doubt that it's a wall, let's see you walk through it. Let's say something happens that activates these old feelings of fear, and you decide to walk right toward it. The closer you get, the more you will have the urge to pull back. That which you collected from your past forms a boundary that you intuitively want to avoid. That's natural, that's what we do with walls; we avoid running into them. But because you avoid running into them, they lock you inside their perimeter. They become your prison because they are the boundaries of your awareness. Because you are not willing to approach them, you cannot see what is beyond them.

When you approach the barrier areas of your thoughts and emotions, it feels like going into an abyss. You don't want to go near that place. But you can go there, and if you want to get out, you will go there. Eventually you will realize that darkness is not what's really there. What is really there are the walls that are blocking the infinite light. When you're looking for light, that is a crucial distinction. If you see a wall and it is protecting you from unending darkness, you will not want to go there. But if you see a wall that is blocking the light, you will want to go there in order to remove the wall. It is often said that you must go through the darkest night in order to get to the infinite light. This is because what we call darkness is really the blockage of light. You must go past these walls.

It's not really difficult to get past the walls. Time and again, every day, the natural flow of life collides with our walls and tries to tear them down. But time and again, we defend them. You must realize that when you defend yourself, you are really defending your walls. There is nothing else to defend in there. There is just your awareness of being and the limited house you built to live in. What you are defending is the house you built to protect yourself. You are hiding inside. If something happens to challenge the walls of your psyche, you get highly defensive. You have built a self-concept, moved inside, and now you defend that home with all you have. But what creates that inner home, other than the walls of your thoughts? When you say, "I'm a woman and I'm forty-five years old. I'm married to Joe and I graduated from this school…" those are thoughts. The actual situations don't exist in there with you except in the form of thoughts that you cling to: "But I was a cheerleader, and I was president of my senior class." That was thirty years ago. Those situations don't exist anymore. But they exist inside of you, and they form the walls in which you live.

What if somebody challenges your self-concept and breaks a little hole in it? What if somebody manages to shake one of those foundational thoughts that the house of your psyche is built upon? Imagine if someone told you when you were twenty years old, "Wait a minute. Those are not your parents. You were adopted. Didn't they ever tell you?" You would adamantly deny it until they showed you the documents. It would shake up your whole inner being. Just one wrong thought and the structure starts to crumble. Tremendous fear and turmoil can open up inside of you simply because something is not the way you thought it was. It shakes you to the core of your being because it challenges the house of thoughts in which you are dwelling. To fix this, you start in with your rationalizations: "I knew they were really nice. They were just like my real parents would've been. Imagine them adopting someone like me and bringing me up just like their own. God, they were even more special than I thought they were." You patched that hole up very well. That's what we do with our walls. We keep them solid. Nothing is allowed to shake those walls.

Notice that you patched the cracking wall with thoughts. You patched with thoughts that which is made of thoughts. That's what we do. Just like the people who fearfully locked themselves inside the dark house in the middle of a sunlit field, and then struggled to create some light, we work hard to build a world within the confines of our inner walls that is better than the inner darkness. We decorate our walls with the memories of our past experiences and with our dreams of the future. In other words, we decorate them with thoughts. But just as the people in the house had the potential to step out of their own self-made, artificial world into the beauty of the natural light, you can step outside your house of thoughts into the unlimited. Your awareness can expand to encompass vast space instead of the limited space in which you dwell. Then, when you look back at that little house you built, you will wonder why you were ever in there.

That is your journey out. True freedom is very close; it's just on the other side of your walls. Enlightenment is a very special thing. But in truth, one should not focus on it. Focus, instead, on the walls of your own making that are blocking the light. Of what purpose is it to build walls that block the light and then strive for enlightenment? You can get out simply by letting everyday life take down the walls you hold around yourself. You simply don't participate in supporting, maintaining, and defending your fortress.

Imagine your house of thoughts standing in the middle of an ocean of light from a trillion stars. Imagine your awareness trapped inside the darkness of that house, struggling daily to live off the artificial light of your limited experiences. Now imagine the walls crumbling down, and the effortless release of consciousness expanding into the brilliance of what is and always was. Now give that experience a name—enlightenment.

CHAPTER 13

far, far beyond

Ultimately, the word "beyond" captures the true meaning of spirituality. In its most basic sense, going beyond means going past where you are. It means not staying in your current state. When you constantly go beyond yourself, there are no more limitations. There are no more boundaries. Limitations and boundaries only exist at the places where you stop going beyond. If you never stop, then you go beyond boundaries, beyond limitations, beyond the sense of a restricted self.

Beyond is infinite in all directions. If you take a laser beam and aim it in any direction, it will go on for infinity. It would only cease to be infinite if you created an artificial boundary that it could not penetrate. Boundaries create the appearance of finiteness in infinite space. Things seem finite because your perception hits mental boundaries. In truth, everything is infinite. It is you who takes that which goes on forever and talks about a mile from here. What is a mile from here? It's nothing but a piece of infinity. There are no limits. There is just the infinite universe.

To go beyond, you must keep going past the limits that you put on things. This requires changes at the core of your being. Right now you are using your analytical mind to break the world up into individual thought objects. You are then using the same mind to put these discrete thoughts together in a defined relationship to each other. You do this in an attempt to feel a semblance of control. This is seen most clearly in your constant attempt to make the unknown known. You say to yourself, "It wouldn't dare rain tomorrow, it's my day off. And since Jennifer loves being outdoors, she will certainly want to go hiking with me. In fact, if I want an extra day off, Tom won't mind covering for me. After all, I covered for him once." You have it all figured out. You know how everything is supposed to be, even the future. Your views, your opinions, your preferences, your concepts, your goals, and your beliefs are all ways of bringing the infinite universe down to the finite where you can feel a sense of control. Since the analytical mind cannot handle the infinite, you created an alternate reality of finite thoughts that can remain fixed within your mind. You have taken the whole, broken it into pieces, and selected a handful of these pieces to be put together in a certain way within your mind. This mental model has become your reality. You must now struggle day and night to make the world fit your model, and you label everything that doesn't fit as wrong, bad, or unfair.

If anything happens that challenges how you view things, you fight. You defend. You rationalize. You get frustrated and angry over simple little things. This is the result of being unable to fit what's actually happening into your model of reality. If you want to go beyond your model, you have to take the risk of not believing in it. If your mental model is bothering you, it's because it doesn't incorporate reality. Your choice is to either resist reality or go beyond the limits of your model.

In order to truly go beyond your model, you must first understand why you built it. The easiest way to understand this is to study what happens when the model doesn't work. Have you ever built your whole world on a model of life predicated upon another person's behavior or the permanence of a relationship? If so, have you ever had that foundation pulled out from under you? Somebody leaves you. Somebody dies. Something goes wrong. Something shakes your model to the core. When this happens, your entire view of who you believe you are, including your relationship to everyone and everything around you, begins to fall apart. You panic and do everything you can to hold it together. You beg, fight, and struggle to try to keep your world from collapsing.

Once you've had an experience like that, and most people have, you realize that the model you've built is tenuous, at best. The entire thing can fall apart. The whole model and all that it's built upon, including your entire view of yourself and everything else, can start to crumble. What you experience when this happens is one of the most important learning experiences of your life. You come face-to-face with what made you build the model. The level of discomfort and disorientation you experience is frightening. You struggle just to get back some semblance of normal perception. What you are really doing is trying to pull the mental model back around you so that you can settle down into your familiar mental setting.

But our whole world doesn't have to fall apart in order for us to see what we're doing in there. We are constantly trying to hold it all together. If you really want to see why you do things, then don't do them and see what happens. Let's say you're a smoker. If you decide to stop smoking, you quickly confront the urges that cause you to smoke. These urges are the reason you smoke. They are the outermost layer of cause. If you can sit through these urges, you will see what caused them. If you can get comfortable with what you see, you will face the next layer of causation, and so on, layer upon layer. Likewise, there's a reason you overeat. There's a reason why you dress the way you do. There's a reason for everything you do. If you want to see why you care so much about what you wear and what your hair is like, then just don't do it one day. Wake up in the morning and go somewhere disheveled with your hair a mess, and see what happens to the energies inside of you. See what happens to you when you don't do the things that make you comfortable. What you'll see is why you're doing them.

You are constantly trying to stay within your comfort zone. You struggle to keep people, places, and things in a manner that supports your model. If they start to go any other way, you get uncomfortable. Your mind then becomes active telling you how to get things back the way you need them to be. The moment somebody starts behaving in a way that is outside your expectations, your mind starts talking. It says, "What should I do about this? I can't just ignore what he did. I could confront him directly or ask someone else to talk to him." Your mind is telling you to fix it. And it doesn't really matter what you end up doing; it's all about getting back within your comfort zone. This zone is finite. All attempts to stay within it keep you finite. Going beyond always means letting go of the effort to keep things within your defined limits.

So there are two ways you can live: you can devote your life to staying in your comfort zone, or you can work on your freedom. In other words, you can devote your whole life to the process of making sure everything fits within your limited model, or you can devote your life to freeing yourself from the limits of your model.

To understand this better, let's take a trip to the zoo. Imagine that you're having a great time until you see a tiger inside a small cage. This causes you to contemplate what it would be like to live the rest of your life in such tight confinement. The very thought is extremely frightening to you. But in truth, the confines of your comfort zone create just such a cage. This inner cage doesn't limit your body; it limits the expanse of your consciousness. Because you are unable to go outside your comfort zone, you are, in essence, locked in confinement.

If you examine this, you will see that you're willing to stay in this cage because you're afraid. Your comfort zone is familiar to you; beyond it is the unknown. To fully appreciate this, just imagine the most paranoid person you have ever met in your entire life. He's so scared. Every moment of his life he thinks somebody's trying to hurt him. If you offer him that tiger's cage, he might accept your offer. He doesn't see it as being locked in a cage. He sees it as protection from what could harm him. That which looks like prison to you, looks like safety to him. What if a security service came to your house and bolted down all the doors and barred all the windows? If you happened to be inside at the time, would you panic and want to get out, or would you thank them for helping you feel safe?

Most people have the second reaction when it comes to the limitations of their psyche. They want to stay in there and feel safe. They don't say, "Get me out of here! I'm locked in this tiny world in which everything has to be a certain way. I have to worry about what everybody's doing, what I look like, and everything I've ever said. I want out." Instead of wanting out, they try to keep their cage stable. If something is not comfortable, they do whatever they must to protect themselves and get back to a feeling of safety. If you've ever done that, it means you love your cage. When the cage of the psyche got rattled, you fixed it so that you could be comfortable inside.

When you truly awake spiritually, you realize you are caged. You wake up and realize that you can hardly move in there. You're constantly hitting the limits of your comfort zone. You see that you're afraid to tell people what you really think. You see that you're too self-conscious to freely express yourself. You see that you have to stay on top of everything in order to be okay.

Why? There's really no reason. You have set these limits on yourself. If you don't stay within them, you get scared, you feel hurt, and you feel threatened. That's your cage. The tiger knows the limits of his cage when he hits the bars. You know the limits of your cage when the psyche starts to resist. Your bars are the outer boundary of your comfort zone. The minute you come to the edge of your cage, it lets you know it in no uncertain terms.

Let's look at this edge by way of an example. In the old days, if you wanted to keep your dog in the backyard, you had to put up a fence. Nowadays you don't need a fence because everything is electronic. You just bury wires underground and put a little collar on the dog. The dog thinks, "Hey, I'm free! I used to have to be inside a fence. This is great!" Of course he goes running right to where he's not supposed to go, and—zap!—he jumps back and barks. What happened? An invisible limit was there, and when the dog approached that limit, it gave him a little shock. It hurt. It was uncomfortable enough so that now the dog feels fear whenever he approaches the boundaries. So you see, a cage doesn't have to look like a cage. It can be a cage created by your fear of discomfort. If you approach your limits, you begin to feel uncomfortable and insecure. Those are the bars of your cage. As long as you stay inside of it, you cannot possibly know what is on the other side. The boundaries of this cage are what make your world appear finite and temporal. The infinite and eternal are just outside the limits of your cage.

Going beyond means going beyond the borders of the cage. There should be no cage. The soul is infinite. It is free to expand everywhere. It is free to experience all of life. This can only happen when you are willing to face reality without mental boundaries. If you still have barriers, and you know what they are because you hit them every day, you must be willing to go beyond them. Otherwise you remain within your cage. And remember, decorating your cage with beautiful experiences, fond memories, and great dreams is not the same as going beyond. A cage by any other name is still a cage. You must be willing to go beyond.

Throughout each day, you frequently hit the edges of your cage. When you hit these edges, you either pull back or try to force things to change so that you can remain comfortable. You actually use the brilliance of your mind to stay inside your cage. Day and night you plot and plan how to stay within your comfort zone. Sometimes you can't even fall asleep at night because you're too busy thinking about what you need to do to stay within your cage: "How can I make it so that she will never leave me? How can I keep her from ever becoming interested in someone else?" You're trying to figure out how to be sure that you won't hit the edges of your cage.

Let's go back to the dog. Since that particular dog was used to roaming free, it's a sad day when he stops trying to get out of the yard. The only reason he would stop trying to go beyond his little space is that he's afraid of the edges. But what if we're dealing with a very brave dog that's determined to be free? Imagine that the dog has not given up. You find him sitting there, right at the place where the collar starts vibrating, and he is not backing off. Every minute he's stepping forward a little bit more in order to get used to the force field. If he continues, he will eventually get out. There's not a chance in the world that he won't. Since it's just an artificial edge, he can get through if he can learn to withstand the discomfort. He just has to be ready, willing, and able to handle the discomfort. The collar cannot actually hurt him; it's just uncomfortable. If he is willing to go beyond his comfort zone, he is free to come and go at will.

Your cage is just like this. When you approach the edges you feel insecurity, jealousy, fear, or self-consciousness. You pull back, and if you are like most people, you stop trying. Spirituality begins when you decide that you'll never stop trying. Spirituality is the commitment to go beyond, no matter what it takes. It's an infinite journey based upon going beyond yourself every minute of every day for the rest of your life. If you're truly going beyond, you are always at your limits. You're never back in the comfort zone. A spiritual being feels as though they are always against that edge, and they are constantly being pushed through it.

Eventually you will realize that it cannot actually hurt you to go beyond your psychological limits. If you are willing to just stand at the edge and keep walking, you will go beyond. You used to pull back when it got uncomfortable. Now you relax and go past that point. That is all it takes to go beyond. Go beyond where you were a minute ago by handling what's happening now.

Would you like to go beyond? Would you like to feel no edges? Imagine a comfort zone that is so expanded that it can easily fit the entire day, no matter what happens. The day unfolds and the mind doesn't say anything. You simply interact with the day with a peaceful, fully inspired heart. If your edges happen to get hit, the mind doesn't complain. It all just passes through. This is how great beings live. When you are trained, like a great athlete, to immediately relax through your edges when they get hit, then it's all over. You realize that you will always be fine. Nothing can ever bother you except your edges, and now you know what to do with them. You end up loving your edges because they point your way to freedom. All you have to do is constantly relax and lean into them. Then one day, when you least expect it, you fall through into the infinite. That is what it means to go beyond.

CHAPTER 14

letting go of false solidity

The inside of one's psyche is a very complex, sophisticated place. It is full of conflicting forces that are constantly changing due to both internal and external stimuli. This results in wide variations of needs, fears, and desires over relatively short periods of time. Because of this, very few people have the clarity to understand what's going on in there. There's just too much happening at once to follow the cause and effect relationships between all of our different thoughts, emotions, and energy levels. As a result, we find ourselves struggling just to hold it all together. But everything keeps on changing—moods, desires, likes, dislikes, enthusiasm, lethargy. It's a full-time task just to maintain the discipline necessary to create even the semblance of control and order in there.

When you're lost and struggling with all these psychological and energetic changes, you are suffering. While it may not seem to you that you're suffering, compared to what it can be, you are suffering. In truth, the very responsibility of having to hold it all together is itself a form of suffering. You notice this most when things start to fall apart outside. Your psyche goes into turmoil, and you have to struggle to hold your inner world together. But what exactly are you trying to hold onto? The only things in there are your thoughts, emotions, and movements of energy, none of which are solid. They are like clouds, simply coming and going through vast inner space. But you keep holding onto them, as though consistency can substitute for stability. The Buddhists have a term for this: "clinging." In the end, clinging is what the psyche is all about.

In order to understand clinging, we must first understand who clings. As you go deeper into yourself, you will naturally come to realize that there is an aspect of your being that is always there and never changes. This is your sense of awareness, your consciousness. It is this awareness that is aware of your thoughts, experiences the ebb and flow of your emotions, and receives your physical senses. This is the root of Self. You are not your thoughts; you are aware of your thoughts. You are not your emotions; you feel your emotions. You are not your body; you look at it in the mirror and experience this world through its eyes and ears. You are the conscious being who is aware that you are aware of all these inner and outer things.

If you explore consciousness, which is your pure sense of awareness, you will see that it really does not exist at any particular point in space. Rather, it is a field of awareness that focuses down to a point by concentrating on a particular set of objects. You can be aware of feeling just one finger, or you can be aware of feeling your entire body at once. You can be totally lost in a single thought, or you can be simultaneously aware of your thoughts, your emotions, your body, and your surroundings. Consciousness is a dynamic field of awareness that has the ability to either narrowly focus or broadly expand. When consciousness concentrates narrowly enough, it loses its broader sense of self. It no longer experiences itself as a field of pure consciousness; it begins to relate itself more to the objects it's focused upon. As we have seen, this is what happens when you get so absorbed in a movie that you completely lose the broader sense of sitting in a cold, dark theater. In this case, you have shifted from concentrating on your body and its surroundings to concentrating on the world of the movie. You literally get lost in the experience. This can be generalized to your entire experience of life. Your sense of self is determined by where you are focusing your consciousness.

But what determines where you focus your consciousness? At the most basic level, it is simply determined by anything that catches your awareness because it stands out from the rest. To understand this, imagine that your consciousness is simply observing vast, empty inner space. Now imagine that passing through this space is the gentle flow of random thought objects: a cat, a horse, a word, a color, or an abstract thought. They are sporadically floating right through your awareness. Now let one object stand out above the rest. It catches your attention and draws the focus of your awareness. You immediately realize that the more focused you become on the object, the slower it moves. Until, eventually, if you focus on it enough, it stops. The force of consciousness ends up holding the object stable simply by concentrating on it. Just as a fish can pass through water but not through ice, which is simply concentrated water, so mental and emotional energy patterns become fixed when they encounter concentrated consciousness. The very act of differentiating the amount of awareness focused on one particular object over any other creates clinging. And the result of clinging is that selective thoughts and emotions stay in one place long enough to become the building blocks of the psyche.

Clinging is one of the most primal acts. Because some objects remain in the consciousness while others pass through, your sense of awareness relates more to them. You use them as fixed points to create a sense of orientation, relationship, and security in the midst of constant inner change. And this need for orientation extends to the outside world. Although you are clinging to inner objects, you use them to orient and relate yourself to the multitude of physical objects that come in through your senses. You then create thoughts that tie all the objects together, and you cling to the entire structure. You actually end up relating so strongly to this inner structure that you build your entire sense of self around it. Because you cling to it, it stays fixed. And because it stays fixed, you relate to it above all else. This is the birth of the psyche. In the midst of the expanse of empty mind, by clinging to passing thought objects, you make an island of apparent solidity. Once you have a thought that stays, you can rest your head on it. Then, as you cling to more and more thoughts, you build an inner structure for consciousness to focus on. The more consciousness narrows its focus onto this mental structure, the greater the tendency to utilize it to define the concept of self. Clinging creates the bricks and mortar with which we build a conceptual self. In the midst of vast inner space, using nothing but the vapor of thoughts, you created a structure of apparent solidity to rest upon.

Who are you that is lost and trying to build a concept of yourself in order to be found? This question represents the essence of spirituality. You will never find yourself in what you have built to define yourself. You're the one who's doing the building. You may assemble the most amazing collection of thoughts and emotions; you may build a truly beautiful, unbelievable, interesting, and dynamic structure; but, obviously, it's not you. You are the one who did this. You are the one who was lost, scared, and confused because you focused your awareness away from your awareness of Self. In this panic, in this lost state, you learned to cling and hold onto the thoughts and emotions that were passing before you. You used them to build a personality, a persona, a self-concept that would allow you to define yourself. Awareness rested itself on the objects it was aware of and called it home. Because you have this model of who you are, it is easier to know how to act, how to make decisions, and how to relate to the outside world. If you dare to look, you will see that you live your entire life based on the model you built around yourself.

Let's get more specific. You try to hold a consistent set of thoughts and concepts in your mind, such as "I am a woman." Yes, even that is a thought, or a concept held in your mind. You, who are holding onto that, are neither male nor female. You are the awareness who hears the thought and sees a woman's body in the mirror. But you cling tightly to these concepts. You think, "I am a woman, I am of a certain age and I believe in one philosophy versus another." You literally define yourself based on what you believe: "I believe in God or I don't believe in God. I believe in peace and nonviolence, or I believe in survival of the fittest. I believe in capitalism, or I believe in neo-socialism." You take a set of thoughts in the mind and you hold onto them. You make a highly complex relational structure out of them, and then present that package as who you are. But it is not who you are. It is just the thoughts you have pulled around yourself in an attempt to define yourself. You do this because you are lost inside.

Basically, you attempt to create a sense of stability and steadiness inside. This generates a false, but welcomed, sense of security. You also want the people around you to have done the same thing. You want people to be steady enough so that you can predict their behavior. If they aren't, it disturbs you. This is because you have made your predictions of their behavior part of your inner model. This protective shield of beliefs and concepts regarding the outside world acts as insulation between you and the people you interact with. By having preconceived notions about other people's behavior, you feel safer and more in control. Imagine the fear you would feel if you let the entire wall down. Who have you ever allowed directly into your true inner self without the protection of your mental buffer? Nobody, not even yourself.

People just put façades out there. They even admit that one façade is a little more real than the other. You go to work and get lost in your professional façade, but then you say, "I'm going home to be with my family and friends where I can just be myself." So your work façade drops into the background, and your relaxed social façade comes forward. But what about you, the one who is holding the façade together? Nobody gets near that one. That's just too scary. That one is too far back there to deal with.

So we are all clinging and then building. Some of us are better at this than others. In most societies you are well rewarded for how good you are at clinging and building. If you get that model down absolutely right, and behave consistently every time, you have actually "created" someone. And if the someone you create is what others want and need, you can be very popular and successful. You are that person. It got engrained in you at a very young age, and you never deviated from it. You can get really good at this game of creating someone. And if the person you created is not receiving the popularity and success you expected, you can adjust your thoughts accordingly. It's not that there is anything wrong with this. Obviously, everybody does it. But who are you that's doing this, and why are you doing it?

It's important to realize that it's not just up to you what thoughts you cling to and what person you create. Society has a lot to say about this. There are acceptable and unacceptable social behaviors for almost everything—how to sit, how to walk, how to speak, how to dress, and how to feel about things. How does our society engrain these mental and emotional structures within us? When you do it well, you are rewarded with hugs and showered with positive accolades. When you don't do it well, you are punished, either physically, mentally, or emotionally.

Just think about how nice you are to people when they behave in accordance with your expectations. Now think about how you close up and pull back from them when they don't. This is not to mention getting angry or even violent toward them. What are you doing? You are trying to change someone's behavior by leaving impressions on their mind. You are attempting to alter their collection of beliefs, thoughts, and emotions so that the next time they act it is in the manner you expect. In truth, we are all doing this to each other every day.

Why do we let this happen to us? Why do we care so much whether other people accept the façade we put out there? It all comes down to understanding why we are clinging to our self-concept. If you stop clinging, you will see why the tendency to cling was there. If you let go of your façade, and don't try to trade it in for a new one, your thoughts and emotions will become unanchored and begin passing through you. It will be a very scary experience. You will feel panic deep inside, and you will be unable to get your bearings. This is what people feel when something very important outside does not fit their inner model. The façade ceases to work and begins to crumble. When it can no longer protect you, you experience great fear and panic. However, you'll find that if you're willing to face that sense of panic, there is a way to go past it. You can go further back into the consciousness that is experiencing it, and the panic will stop. Then there will be a great peace, like nothing you've ever felt.

That's the part very few people come to know: it can stop. The noise, the fear, the confusion, the constant changing of these inner energies—it can all stop. You thought you had to protect yourself, so you grabbed onto the things that were coming at you and used them to hide. You took what you could get your hands on, and you started to cling in order to build solidity. But you can let go of what you're clinging to and not play this game. You just have to take the risk of letting it all go and daring to face the fear that was driving you. Then you can pass through that part of you, and it will all be over. It will stop—no more struggling, just peace.

This journey is one of passing through exactly where you have been struggling not to go. As you pass through that state of turmoil, the consciousness itself is your only repose. You will just be aware that tremendous changes are taking place. You will be aware that there is no solidity and you will become comfortable with that. You will be aware that each moment of each day is unfolding and you neither have control, nor crave it. You have no concepts, no hopes, no dreams, no beliefs, and no security. You are no longer building mental models of what's going on, but life is going on anyway. You are perfectly comfortable just being aware of it. Here comes this moment, then the next moment, and then the next. But that's really what has always happened. Moment after moment has been passing before your consciousness. The difference is that now you see it happening. You see that your emotions and your mind are reacting to these moments that are coming through, and you're doing nothing to stop it. You're doing nothing to control it. You're just letting life unfold, both outside and inside of you.

If you take this journey, you will get to the state in which you see exactly how the unfolding moments bring up a sense of fear. From this place of clarity, you will be able to experience the powerful tendency to protect yourself. This tendency exists because you truly have no control, and that is not comfortable to you. But if you really want to break through, you have to be willing to just watch the fear without protecting yourself from it. You must be willing to see that this need to protect yourself is where the entire personality comes from. It was created by building a mental and emotional structure to get away from that sense of fear. You are now standing face-to-face with the root of the psyche.

If you go deep enough, you can watch the psyche being built. You will see that you are in the middle of nowhere, in empty infinite space, and all of these inner objects are flowing toward you. Thoughts, feelings, and the impressions of worldly experiences are all pouring into your consciousness. You will clearly see that the tendency is to protect yourself from this flow by bringing it under your control. There is an overwhelmingly strong tendency to lean forward and grab onto selective impressions of people, places, and things as they flow through. You will see that if you focus on these mental images, they become part of a complex structure where there was none. You will see events that took place when you were ten years old that you're still holding onto. You will see that you're literally taking all your memories, pulling them together in an orderly fashion, and saying that's who you are. But you are not the events; you're the one who experienced the events. How can you define yourself as the things that happened to you? You were aware of your existence before they happened. You are the one who is in there doing all this, seeing all this, and experiencing all this. You do not have to cling to your experiences in the name of building yourself. This is a false self you are building inside. It is just a concept of yourself that you hide behind.

How long have you been hiding in there struggling to keep it all together? Any time anything goes wrong in the protective model you built about yourself, you defend and rationalize in order to get it back together. Your mind does not stop struggling until you've processed the event or somehow made it go away. People feel their very existence is at stake, and they will fight and argue until they get control back. This is all because we have attempted to build solidity where there is none. Now we have to fight to keep it together. The problem is, there is no way out that way. There is no peace and there is no winning in that struggle. You were told not to build your house upon sand. Well, this is the ultimate sand. In fact, you built your house in empty space. If you continue to cling to what you built, you will have to continually and perpetually defend yourself. You will have to keep everybody and everything straight in order to reconcile your conceptual model with reality. It's a constant struggle to keep it together.

What it means to live spiritually is to not participate in this struggle. It means that the events that happen in the moment belong to the moment. They don't belong to you. They have nothing to do with you. You must stop defining yourself in relationship to them, and just let them come and go. Don't allow events to leave impressions inside of you. If you find yourself thinking about them later on, just let go. If an event happens that doesn't fit your conceptual model, and you see yourself struggling and rationalizing to make it fit, just notice what you're doing. An event in the universe didn't match your model and it's causing disturbance inside of you. If you will simply notice this, you will find that it is actually breaking up your model. You'll get to the point where you like this because you don't want to keep your model. You'll define this as good because you are no longer willing to put any energy into building and solidifying your façade. Instead, you will actually permit the things that disturb your model to act as the dynamite to break it up and free you. This is what it means to live spiritually.

When you become truly spiritual, you are totally different from everybody else. That which everybody else wants, you don't want. That which everybody else resists, you totally accept. You want your model to break, and you honor the experience when something happens that can cause disturbance within you. Why should anything that anyone says or does cause you to get disturbed? You're just on a planet spinning around the middle of absolutely nowhere. You came here to visit for a handful of years and then you're going to leave. How can you live all stressed-out over everything? Don't do it. If anything can cause disturbance inside of you, it means it hit your model. It means it hit the false part of you that you built in order to control your own definition of reality. But if that model is reality, why didn't experiential reality fit? There's nothing you can make up inside your mind that can ever be considered reality.

You must learn to be comfortable with psychological disturbance. If your mind becomes hyperactive, just watch it. If your heart starts to heat up, let it go through what it must. Try to find the part of you that is capable of noticing that your mind is hyperactive and that your heart is heating up. That part is your way out. There is no way out through building this model of yours. The only way to inner freedom is through the one who watches: the Self. The Self simply notices that the mind and emotions are unraveling, and that nothing is struggling to hold them together.

Of course this will be painful. The reason you built the whole mental structure was to avoid pain. If you let it fall apart, you're going to feel the pain that you were avoiding when you built it. You must be willing to face this pain. If you were to lock yourself in a fortress because you were afraid to come out, you would have to face that fear if you ever wanted to experience a fuller existence. That fortress would not be protecting you; it would be imprisoning you. To be free, to truly experience life, you must come out. You have to let go and pass through the cleansing process that frees you from your psyche. You do this by simply watching the psyche be the psyche. The way out is through awareness. Stop defining the disturbed mind as a negative experience; just see if you can relax behind it. When your mind is disturbed, don't ask, "What do I do about this?" Instead ask, "Who am I that notices this?"

In time, you will come to realize that the center from which you watch disturbance cannot get disturbed. If it appears disturbed, just notice who is noticing that disturbance. Eventually it will stop. You will then be able to rest back into the depths of your being while watching your mind and heart create their last throes of turmoil. When you reach that point, you will understand what it means to be transcendent. Awareness transcends what it is aware of. It is as separate as light is from what it shines upon. You are consciousness, and you can free yourself from all of this by relaxing behind it.

If you want permanent peace, permanent joy, and permanent happiness, you have to get through to the other side of the inner turmoil. You can experience a life in which waves of love can rush up inside of you any time you want. It is the nature of your being. You simply have to go to the other side of the psyche. You do that by letting go of the tendency to cling. You do it by not using your mind to build false solidity. You just decide, once and for all, to take the journey by constantly letting go.

At this point, the journey becomes very quick. You will go through the part of you that has always been scared to death, and you'll see how that part has always struggled to hold it all together. If you don't feed that part, if you just keep letting go and don't let it cling, eventually you will fall behind the false solidity. This is not something you do; it is something that happens to you.

Your only way out is the witness. Just keep letting go by being aware that you are aware. If you pass through a period of darkness or depression, just ask, "Who is aware of the darkness?" That's how you pass through the different stages of your inner growth. You just keep letting go, and remain aware that you are still there. When you've let go of the dark psyche, and you've let go of the light psyche, and you're no longer clinging to anything, you will reach a point where it will all open up behind you. You are used to being aware of things in front of you. You now become aware of a universe behind your seat of consciousness.

It didn't look like there was anything behind you. Because you were so focused on building your model out of the thoughts and emotions passing before you, there was no awareness of the vast expanse of space inside. Back behind, there is a whole universe. You're just not looking that way. If you're willing to let go, you'll fall back and it will open into an ocean of energy. You will become filled with light. You will become filled with a light that has no darkness, with a peace that passeth all understanding. You will then walk through every moment of your daily life with the flow of this inner force sustaining you, feeding you, and guiding you from deep within. You will still have thoughts, emotions, and a self-concept floating around in inner space, but they will be just one small part of what you experience. You will not identify with anything outside the sense of Self.

Once you reach this state, you will never have to worry about anything ever again. The forces of creation will create creation, both inside and outside of you. You will float in peace, love, and compassion beyond it all, yet honoring it all. There is no need for false solidity when you are at peace with the universal expanse of your true Being.

PART V

living life

Photo (previous page)
Apollo 11 Earthrise
Image credit: NASA JSC

CHAPTER 15

the path of unconditional happiness

The highest spiritual path is life itself. If you know how to live daily life, it all becomes a liberating experience. But first you have to approach life properly, or it can be very confusing. To begin with, you have to realize that you really only have one choice in this life, and it's not about your career, whom you want to marry, or whether you want to seek God. People tend to burden themselves with so many choices. But, in the end, you can throw it all away and just make one basic, underlying decision: Do you want to be happy, or do you not want to be happy? It's really that simple. Once you make that choice, your path through life becomes totally clear.

Most people don't dare give themselves that choice because they think it's not under their control. Someone might say, "Well, of course I want to be happy, but my wife left me." In other words, they want to be happy, but not if their wife leaves them. But that wasn't the question. The question was, very simply, "Do you want to be happy or not?" If you keep it that simple, you will see that it really is under your control. It's just that you have a deep-seated set of preferences that gets in the way.

Let's say you've been lost and without food for days, and you finally find your way to a house. You can hardly make it to the doorstep, but you manage to pull yourself up and knock on the door. Somebody opens the door, looks at you and says, "Oh my God! You poor thing! Do you want something to eat? What would you like?" Now the truth is, you really don't care what they give you. You don't even want to think about it. You just utter the word "food." And because you really mean it when you say you need food, it no longer has anything to do with your mental preferences. The same goes for the question about happiness. The question is simply "Do you want to be happy?" If the answer is really yes, then say it without qualifying it. After all, what the question really means is "Do you want to be happy from this point forward for the rest of your life, regardless of what happens?"

Now, if you say yes, it might happen that your wife leaves you, or your husband dies, or the stock market crashes, or your car breaks down on an open highway at night. Those things might happen between now and the end of your life. But if you want to walk the highest spiritual path, then when you answer yes to that simple question, you must really mean it. There are no ifs, ands, or buts about it. It's not a question of whether your happiness is under your control. Of course it's under your control. It's just that you don't really mean it when you say you're willing to stay happy. You want to qualify it. You want to say that as long as this doesn't happen, or as long as that does happen, then you're willing to be happy. That's why it seems like it is out of your control.

Any condition you create will limit your happiness. You simply aren't going to be able to control things and keep them the way you want them.

You have to give an unconditional answer. If you decide that you're going to be happy from now on for the rest of your life, you will not only be happy, you will become enlightened. Unconditional happiness is the highest technique there is. You don't have to learn Sanskrit or read any scriptures. You don't have to renounce the world. You just have to really mean it when you say that you choose to be happy. And you have to mean it regardless of what happens. This is truly a spiritual path, and it is as direct and sure a path to Awakening as could possibly exist.

Once you decide you want to be unconditionally happy, something inevitably will happen that challenges you. This test of your commitment is exactly what stimulates spiritual growth. In fact, it is the unconditional aspect of your commitment that makes this the highest path. It's so simple. You just have to decide whether or not you will break your vow. When everything is going well, it's easy to be happy. But the moment something difficult happens, it's not so easy. You tend to find yourself saying, "But I didn't know this was going to happen. I didn't think I'd miss my flight. I didn't think Sally would show up at the party wearing the same dress that

I had on. I didn't think that somebody would dent my brand-new car one hour after I got it." Are you really willing to break your vow of happiness because these events took place?

Billions of things could happen that you haven't even thought of yet. The question is not whether they will happen. Things are going to happen. The real question is whether you want to be happy regardless of what happens. The purpose of your life is to enjoy and learn from your experiences. You were not put on Earth to suffer. You're not helping anybody by being miserable. Regardless of your philosophical beliefs, the fact remains that you were born and you are going to die. During the time in between, you get to choose whether or not you want to enjoy the experience. Events don't determine whether or not you're going to be happy. They're just events. You determine whether or not you're going to be happy. You can be happy just to be alive. You can be happy having all these things happen to you, and then be happy to die. If you can live this way, your heart will be so open and your Spirit will be so free, that you will soar up to the heavens.

This path leads you to absolute transcendence because any part of your being that would add a condition to your commitment to happiness has got to go. If you want to be happy, you have to let go of the part of you that wants to create melodrama. This is the part that thinks there's a reason not to be happy. You have to transcend the personal, and as you do, you will naturally awaken to the higher aspects of your being.

In the end, enjoying life's experiences is the only rational thing to do. You're sitting on a planet spinning around in the middle of absolutely nowhere. Go ahead, take a look at reality. You're floating in empty space in a universe that goes on forever. If you have to be here, at least be happy and enjoy the experience. You're going to die anyway. Things are going to happen anyway. Why shouldn't you be happy? You gain nothing by being bothered by life's events. It doesn't change the world; you just suffer. There's always going to be something that can bother you, if you let it.

This choice to enjoy life will lead you through your spiritual journey. In truth, it is itself a spiritual teacher. Committing yourself to unconditional happiness will teach you every single thing there is to learn about yourself, about others, and about the nature of life. You will learn all about your mind, your heart, and your will. But you have to mean it when you say that you'll be happy for the rest of your life. Every time a part of you begins to get unhappy, let it go. Work with it. Use affirmations, or do whatever you need to do to stay open. If you are committed, nothing can stop you. No matter what happens, you can choose to enjoy the experience. If they starve you and put you in solitary confinement, just have fun being like Gandhi. No matter what happens, just enjoy the life that comes to you.

As difficult as that sounds, what's the benefit of not doing it? If you're totally innocent and they lock you up, you might as well have fun. What good does it do to not have fun? It doesn't change anything. In the end, if you stay happy, you win. Make that your game, and just stay happy no matter what.

The key to staying happy is really very simple. Begin by understanding your inner energies. If you look inside, you will see that when you're happy, your heart feels open and the energy rushes up inside of you. When you aren't happy, your heart feels closed and no energy comes up inside. So to stay happy, just don't close your heart. No matter what happens, even if your wife leaves you or your husband dies, you don't close.

There is no rule that says you have to close. Just tell yourself that no matter what happens, you're not going to close. You really do have that choice. When you start to close, just question if you're really willing to give up your happiness. You should examine what it is inside of you that believes there's some benefit to closing. The slightest thing happens to you, and you give away your happiness. You were having a great day until someone cut you off on your way to work. It got you really upset and you stayed that way the rest of the day. Why? Dare to ask yourself that question. What good came from letting it ruin your day? There was no benefit. If somebody cuts you off, let go and stay open. If you really want to, you can.

If you take on this path of unconditional happiness, you will go through all of the various stages of yoga. You will have to stay conscious, centered, and committed at all times. You will have to stay one-pointed on your commitment to remain open and receptive to life. But nobody said that you can't do this. Staying open is what the great saints and masters taught. They taught that God is joy, God is ecstasy, and God is love. If you remain open enough, waves of uplifting energy will fill your heart. Spiritual practices are not an end in themselves. They bear fruit when you become deep enough to remain open. If you learn to stay open at all times, great things will happen to you. You simply have to learn not to close.

The key is to learn to keep your mind disciplined enough so that it doesn't trick you into thinking that this time it's worth closing. If you slip, get back up. The minute you slip, the minute you open your mouth, the minute you start to close and defend yourself, get back up. Just pick yourself up and affirm inwardly that you don't want to close, no matter what happens. Affirm that all you want is to be at peace and to appreciate life. You don't want your happiness to be conditional upon the behavior of other people. It's bad enough that your happiness is conditional upon your own behavior. When you start making it conditional upon other people's behavior, you're in serious trouble.

Things are going to happen to you, and you're going to feel the tendency to close. But you have the choice to either go with it or let it go. Your mind will tell you that it's not reasonable to stay open when these things happen. But you have limited time left in your life, and what's really not reasonable is to not enjoy life.

If you have trouble remembering that, then meditate. Meditation strengthens your center of consciousness so that you're always aware enough to not allow your heart to close. You remain open by simply letting go and releasing the tendency to close. You just relax your heart when it starts to tighten. You don't have to be outwardly glowing all the time; you're just joyful inside. Instead of complaining, you're just having fun with the different situations that unfold.

Unconditional happiness is a very high path and a very high technique because it solves everything. You could learn yoga techniques, such as meditation and postures, but what do you do with the rest of your life? The technique of unconditional happiness is ideal because what you're doing with the rest of your life is already defined—you're letting go of yourself so that you can remain happy. As far as your spirituality goes, you're going to grow very rapidly. A person who actually does this every moment of every day is going to notice the cleansing of their heart. This is because they're not getting involved in the stuff that comes up. They're also going to notice the purification of their mind because they are not getting involved in the mind's melodrama. Their Shakti (Spirit) is going to awaken even if they know nothing about Shakti. They will come to know a happiness that is beyond human understanding. This path solves daily life and it solves spiritual life. The greatest gift one can give to God is to be pleased with His creation.

Do you think God likes to be around people that are happy or people that are miserable? It's not hard to tell. Just think about it by imagining that you're God. You created the heavens and earth so that you can play and experience yourself, and now you're dropping down to check on your humans. So God asks the first human He sees,

"How are you doing?"

The human says, "What do you mean, how am I doing?"

The Path of Unconditional Happiness

"Well, do you like it here?"

"No, I don't like it here."

"Why not? What's wrong?"

"That tree is bent in five places; I want it to be straight. This person went out with somebody else, and that person ran up a hundred-dollar phone bill. This person has a nicer car than mine and that person dresses funny. It's just terrible. Plus my nose is too big, my ears are too small, and my toes are weird. I'm not happy with it. I don't like any of it."

So God says, "Well, how about the animals?"

"The animals? The ants and mosquitoes bite you; it's a terrible thing. I can't go out at night because there are all these animals out there. They howl and poop all over the place, and I just don't like it."

Do you think God likes listening to this? He says, "What do you think—I'm a complaint department?" Then He goes and visits somebody else, and again, He asks,

"How are you doing?"

This person says, "I'm ecstatic."

God says, "Wow! Well, how do you like things?"

"They're beautiful. Everything I look at just creates waves of joy inside me. I look at that bent tree; it just blows me away. The ant comes and bites me, and it's just so amazing that a tiny ant could be brave enough to bite a giant like me!"

Now you guess who God wants to hang out with. One of the ancient names for God in the yogic tradition is *Satchitananda*—Eternal, Conscious Bliss. God is ecstasy. God is as high as it gets. If you want to be close to God, learn to be joyful. If you remain spontaneously happy and centered, no matter what happens, you will find God. That's the amazing part. Yes, you will find happiness, but that's nothing compared to what you're really going to find.

Once you have passed through trial by fire, and you are thoroughly convinced that you will let go no matter what, then the veils of the human mind and heart will fall away. You will stand face-to-face with what is beyond you because there is no longer a need for you. When you are done playing with the temporal and finite, you will open to the eternal and infinite. Then the word "happiness" can't describe your state. That's where words like ecstasy, bliss, liberation, Nirvana, and freedom come in. The joy becomes overwhelming, and your cup runneth over.

This is a beautiful path. Be happy.

CHAPTER 16

the spiritual path of nonresistance

One should view their spiritual work as learning to live life without stress, problems, fear, or melodrama. This path of using life to evolve spiritually is truly the highest path. There really is no reason for tension or problems. Stress only happens when you resist life's events. If you're neither pushing life away, nor pulling it toward you, then you are not creating any resistance. You are simply present. In this state, you are just witnessing and experiencing the events of life taking place. If you choose to live this way, you will see that life can be lived in a state of peace.

What an amazing process life is, this flow of atoms through time and space. It's just an eternal sequence of events that take form and then instantly dissolve into the next moment. If you resist this amazing force of life, tension builds within you and gets into your body, mind, and spiritual heart.

It is not difficult to see the tendency toward stress and resistance in daily life. But if we want to understand this tendency, we must first examine why we are so resistant to just letting life be life. What is it inside of us that even has the ability to resist the reality of life? If you look carefully inside yourself, you will see that it's you, the Self, the indwelling being, that has this power. It is called willpower.

The Spiritual Path of Nonresistance

Will is a real force that emanates from your being. It is what makes your arms and legs move. They don't just move randomly by themselves. They move the way they do because you assert will to make them do so. You use the same will to hold onto thoughts when you want to concentrate on them. The power of Self, when it is concentrated and directed into the physical, mental, or emotional realms, creates a force, and we call that force "will." That's what you use when you try to make things happen or not happen. You are not helpless in there; you have the power to affect things.

It's amazing to see what we end up doing with our will. We actually assert our will in opposition to the flow of life. If something happens that we don't like, we resist it. But since what we're resisting has already taken place, what good is it to resist? If your best friend moves away, it's understandable that you don't like it. But your inner resistance to that event for years to come does not change the fact that they did, indeed, move away. It does not do anything to the reality of the situation.

The fact is, it cannot even be argued that we're resisting the actual situation. For instance, if somebody says something that we don't like, obviously our resistance won't stop them from having said it. What we're really resisting is the experience of the event passing through us. We don't want it affecting us inside. We know it is going to make mental and emotional impressions that will not fit with what's already in there. So we assert the force of will against the influence of the event in an attempt to stop it from passing through our hearts and minds. In other words, the experience of an event does not stop with our sensory observation of it. The event also has to pass through the psyche at an energetic level. This is a process we experience every day. The initial sensory observation touches our mental and emotional energy pools, creating movements in the energy. These movements pass through the psyche much like physical impact ripples through water. Amazingly, you actually have the ability to resist these movements of energy. The assertion of willpower can stop the energy transfer, and that's what creates tension. You can wear yourself out struggling with the experience of a single event, or even a single thought or emotion. And you know that all too well.

Eventually you'll see that this resistance is a tremendous waste of energy. The fact is, you're generally using your will to resist one of two things: that which has already happened or that which hasn't happened yet. You are sitting inside resisting impressions from the past or thoughts about the future. Think of how much energy is wasted resisting what has already happened. Since the event has already passed, you are actually struggling with yourself, not with the event. In addition, contemplate how much energy is wasted resisting what might happen. Since most of the things you think might happen never do, you are just throwing your energy away.

How you deal with your energy flow has a major effect on your life. If you assert your will against the energy of an event that has already happened, it is like trying to stop the ripples caused by a leaf dropped into a still lake. Anything you do causes more disturbance, not less. When you resist, the energy has no place to go. It gets stuck in your psyche and seriously affects you. It blocks your heart's energy flow and causes you to feel closed and less vibrant. This is literally what is happening when something is weighing on your mind or when things just get too heavy for you.

This is the human predicament. Events have happened and we continue to hold their energy inside of us by resisting them. Now, when we face today's events, we are neither prepared to receive them nor capable of digesting them. This is because we're still struggling with past energies. Over time, the energies can build up to the point that a person becomes so blocked that they either blow up or shut down completely. This is what it means to get stressed-out or even totally burned-out.

There is no reason to get stressed-out. There is no reason for blowing up or shutting down. If you do not let this energy build up inside you, but instead allow each moment of each day to pass through you, then you can be as fresh every moment as you would be on a stress-free vacation. It is not life's events that are causing problems or stress. It is your resistance to life's events that is causing this experience. Since the problem is caused by using your will to resist the reality of life passing through you, the solution is quite obvious—stop resisting. If you are going to resist something, at least have some rational basis for resisting. Otherwise, you are irrationally wasting precious energy.

Be willing to examine the process of resistance. In order to resist you first must decide that something is not the way you like it. Plenty of events make it right through you. Why did you decide to resist this one? Something inside of you must have a basis for deciding when to simply let things pass through and when to assert willpower to either push them away or cling to them. There are a billion things that don't bother you at all. You drive to work every day and you hardly notice the buildings and trees. The white lines on the road don't stress you out at all. You see them, but they pass right through you. Don't assume, however, it's that way for everyone. Someone who paints street lines for a living could get very stressed-out if those white lines were not even. In fact, they could get so stressed-out that they refuse to drive down that road anymore. It's clear that not all of us resist the same things or have the same issues. This is because we don't all have the same preconceived notions of how things should be or how much they should matter to us.

If you want to understand stress, begin by realizing that you carry around with you your own set of preconceived notions of how things should be. It is based upon these notions that you assert your will to resist what has already happened. Where did you get these preconceived notions? Let's say that seeing azaleas in bloom stresses you out. Surely that doesn't bother most people. Why does it bother you? All we need to know is that you once had a girlfriend who grew azaleas, and she broke up with you when they were in bloom. Now every time you see azaleas in bloom, your heart closes. You don't even want to go near the things; they just create too much disturbance for you.

These personal events that take place in our lives leave impressions on our minds and hearts. Those impressions become the basis for asserting our will to either resist or cling. It's no deeper than that. The events may have happened in your childhood or at various points throughout your life. Regardless of when they happened, they left impressions inside of you. Now, based on these past impressions, you are resisting the current events that are taking place. This creates inner tension, turmoil, struggle, and suffering. Instead of seeing this and refusing to allow these past events to run your life, you buy into them. Believing they have real meaning, you put all your heart and soul into either resisting or clinging. But in truth, this entire process has no real meaning. It just destroys your life.

The alternative is to use life to let go of these impressions and the stress they create. In order to do this you have to become very conscious. You have to carefully watch the mental voice that tells you to resist something. It literally commands you: "I don't like what he said. Fix it." It gives you advice and tells you to confront the world by resisting things. Why do you listen to it? Let your spiritual path become the willingness to let whatever happens make it through you, rather than carrying it into the next moment. That doesn't mean you don't deal with what happens. You're welcome to deal with it, but first let the energy make it through you. If you don't, you will not actually be dealing with the current event, you will be dealing with your own blocked energies from the past. You will not be coming from a place of clarity, but from a place of inner resistance and tension.

To avoid this, begin dealing with each situation with acceptance. Acceptance means that events can make it through you without resistance. If an event takes place and is able to make it through your psyche, you will be left face-to-face with the actual situation as it truly exists. Since you are dealing with the actual event, rather than stored energies stimulated by the event, you won't assert reactive energy from your past. You will find that you are able to deal with daily situations much better. It is actually possible to never have another problem for the rest of your life. This is because events are not problems; they're just events. Your resistance to them is what causes the problem. But, again, don't think that because you accept reality it means you don't deal with things. You do deal with them. You just deal with them as events that are taking place on the planet Earth, and not as personal problems.

You will be surprised to find that in most situations there's nothing to deal with except for your own fears and desires. Fear and desire make everything seem so complicated. If you don't have fear or desire about an event, there's really nothing to deal with. You simply allow life to unfold and interact with it in a natural and rational manner. When the next thing happens, you're fully present in that moment and simply enjoying the experience of life. There are no problems. It's all about no problems, no tension, no stress, and no burnout. When the events of this world make it through you, you have reached a deep spiritual state. You can then be conscious in the presence of whatever takes place, without building up blocked energies. When you attain that state, everything becomes clear. In contrast, everybody else is attempting to deal with the world around them while struggling with their own reactions and personal preferences. When a person is dealing with their own fears, anxieties, and desires, how much energy is left for dealing with what's actually happening?

Stop and think about what you're capable of achieving. Up to now, your capacities have been constrained by constant inner struggles. Imagine what would happen if your awareness was free to focus only on the events actually taking place. You would have no noise going on inside. If you lived like this, you could do anything. Your capabilities would be exponential compared to what you've ever experienced. If you could bring this level of awareness and clarity to everything you do, your life would change.

So, as your path, you take on the work of using life to let go of your resistance. Relationships are a great way to work with yourself. Imagine if you used relationships to get to know other people, rather than to satisfy what is blocked inside of you. If you're not trying to make people fit into your preconceived notions of what you like and dislike, you will find that relationships are not really that difficult. If you're not so busy judging and resisting people based upon what is blocked inside of you, you will find that they are much easier to get along with—and so are you. Letting go of yourself is the simplest way to get closer to others.

The same is true in your daily work. Daily work is fun. In fact, it's easy. Your work is just what you do with yourself during the day while you're spinning on a planet through empty space. If you want to be content and enjoy your work, you have to let go of yourself and let events flow through you. Your real work is what is left to do after all else passes through.

Once the personal energies pass through you, the world becomes a different place. People and events will appear different to you. You will realize that you have talents and abilities you never saw before. Your whole view of life will change. Every single thing in this world will look like it's been transformed. This happens because as you let go in one situation, it affects your clarity for other situations. For example, let's say you're afraid of dogs. You come to realize that other people aren't afraid, and they make it through life. Since you've been afraid your whole life, you suffered while others didn't. That suffering had no meaning. So you decide to work with your fear and relax when you see a dog. The way to work with resistance is by relaxing. That act of relaxing through your personal resistance not only changes your relationship with dogs, it changes your relationship with everything. Your soul has now learned how to let disturbing energies pass through. The next time somebody says or does something you don't like, you automatically treat it the same as you did the fear of dogs. This process of relaxing through resistance is beneficial to everything in your life. This is because it directly addresses how to keep your heart open when it is trying to close.

Deep inner release is a spiritual path in and of itself. It is the path of nonresistance, the path of acceptance, the path of surrender. It's about not resisting energies as they pass through you. If you have difficulty doing this, don't get down on yourself. Just keep working with it. It's the work of a lifetime to become that open, that complete, and that whole.

The key is to just relax and release, and deal only with what's left in front of you. You do not need to worry about the rest. If you relax and release, you will see that it puts you through tremendous spiritual growth. You'll start to feel an enormous amount of energy awaken inside of you. You will feel much more love than you've ever felt before. You will feel more peace and contentment, and eventually nothing will ever disturb you again.

You truly can reach a state in which you never have any more stress, tension, or problems for the rest of your life. You just have to realize that life is giving you a gift, and that gift is the flow of events that takes place between your birth and your death. These events are exciting, challenging, and create tremendous growth. To comfortably handle this flow of life, your heart and mind must be open and expansive enough to encompass reality. The only reason they're not is because you resist. Learn to stop resisting reality, and what used to look like stressful problems will begin to look like the stepping-stones of your spiritual journey.

contemplating death

It is truly a great cosmic paradox that one of the best teachers in all of life turns out to be death. No person or situation could ever teach you as much as death has to teach you. While someone could tell you that you are not your body, death shows you. While someone could remind you of the insignificance of the things that you cling to, death takes them all away in a second. While people can teach you that men and women of all races are equal and that there is no difference between the rich and the poor, death instantly makes us all the same.

The question is, are you going to wait until that last moment to let death be your teacher? The mere possibility of death has the power to teach us at any moment. A wise person realizes that at any moment they may breathe out, and the breath may not come back in. It could happen any time, in any place, and your last breath is gone. You have to learn from this. A wise being completely and totally embraces the reality, the inevitability, and the unpredictability of death.

Any time you're having trouble with something, think of death. Let's say you're the jealous type, and you can't stand anyone being close to your mate. Think about what will happen when you're no longer here. Is it really all that romantic that your loved one should live alone with no one to care for them? If you can get past your personal issues, you'll find that you want the person you love to be happy and to have a full and beautiful life. Since that is what you want for them, why are you bothering them now just for talking to someone?

It shouldn't take death to challenge you to live at your highest level. Why wait until everything is taken from you before you learn to dig down deep inside yourself to reach your highest potential? A wise person affirms, "If with one breath all of this can change, then I want to live at the highest level while I'm alive. I'm going to stop bothering the people I love. I'm going to live life from the deepest part of my being."

This is the consciousness necessary for deep and meaningful relationships. Look how callous we get with our loved ones. We take it for granted that they're there and that they'll continue to be there for us. What if they died? What if you died? What if you knew that this evening would be the last time you'd get to see them? Imagine that an angel comes down and tells you, "Straighten up your affairs. You will not awake from your sleep tonight. You're coming to me." Then you'd know that every person you see that day, you'd be seeing for the last time. How would you feel? How would you interact with them? Would you even bother with the little grudges and complaints you've been carrying around? How much love could you give the ones you love, knowing it would be the last time you'd get to be with them? Think about what it would be like if you lived like that every moment with everyone. Your life would be really different. You should contemplate this. Death is not a morbid thought. Death is the greatest teacher in all of life.

Take a moment to look at the things you think you need. Look at how much time and energy you put into various activities. Imagine if you knew you were going to die within a week or a month. How would that change things? How would your priorities change? How would your thoughts change? Think honestly about what you would do with your last week. What a wonderful thought to contemplate. Then ponder this question: If that's really what you would do with your last week, what are you doing with the rest of your time? Wasting it? Throwing it away? Treating it like it's not something precious? What are you doing with life? That is what death asks you.

Let's say you're living life without the thought of death, and the Angel of Death comes to you and says, "Come, it's time to go." You say, "But no. You're supposed to give me a warning so I can decide what I want to do with my last week. I'm supposed to get one more week." Do you know what Death will say to you? He'll say, "My God! I gave you fifty-two weeks this past year alone. And look at all the other weeks I've given you. Why would you need one more? What did you do with all those?" If asked that, what are you going to say? How will you answer? "I wasn't paying attention… I didn't think it mattered." That's a pretty amazing thing to say about your life.

Death is a great teacher. But who lives with that level of awareness? It doesn't matter what age you are; at any time you could take a breath and there may never be another. It happens all the time—to babies, to teenagers, to people in mid-life—not just to the aged. One breath and they're gone. No one knows when their time will be. That's not how it works.

So why not be bold enough to regularly reflect on how you would live that last week? If you were to ask this question of people who are truly awakened, they wouldn't have any problem answering you. Not a thing would change inside of them. Not a thought would cross their minds. If death were to come in an hour, if death were to come in a week, or if death were to come in a year, they would live exactly the same way as they're living now. There is not a single thing they carry inside of their hearts that they would rather be doing. In other words, they are living their lives fully and are not making compromises or playing games with themselves.

You have to be willing to look at what it would be like if death was staring you in the face. Then you have to come to peace within yourself so that it doesn't make any difference whether it is or not. There is a story of a great yogi who said that every moment of his life he felt as though a sword were suspended above his head by a spiderweb. He lived his life with the awareness that he was that close to death. You are that close to death. Every time you get in the car, every time you walk across the street, and every time you eat something, it could be the last thing you do. Do you realize that what you're doing at any moment is something that someone was doing when they died? "He died eating dinner… He died in a car accident, two miles from his home… She died in a plane wreck on a trip to New York… He went to bed and never woke up…" At some point, this is how it happened to somebody. No matter what you're doing, you can be sure somebody died that way.

You must not be afraid to discuss death. Don't get uptight about it. Instead, let this knowledge help you to live every moment of your life fully, because every moment matters. That's what happens when somebody knows they only have a week left. You can be certain that they would tell you that the most important week they ever had was that last week. Everything is a million times more meaningful in that final week. What if you were to live every week that way?

At this point you should ask yourself why you aren't living that way. You are going to die. You know that. You just don't know when. Every single thing will be taken from you. You will leave behind your possessions, your loved ones, and all your hopes and dreams for this life. You'll be taken right out of where you are. You'll no longer be able to fill the roles you were so busy playing. Death changes everything in a flash. That's the reality of the situation. If all these things can be changed in an instant, then maybe they aren't so real after all. Maybe you'd better check out who you are. Maybe you should look deeper.

The beauty of embracing deep truths is that you don't have to change your life; you just change how you live your life. It's not what you're doing; it's how much of you is doing it. Let's take a very simple example. You've walked outside thousands of times, but how many times have you really appreciated it? Imagine a person in a hospital bed who has just been told they've got a week to live. They look up at the doctor and say, "Can I walk outside? Can I look at the sky just one more time?" If it were raining outside, they would want to feel the rain just once more. For them, that would be the most precious thing. But you don't want to feel the rain. You run and cover up.

What is it that won't let us live our lives? What is inside of us that is so afraid that it keeps us from just enjoying life? This part of us is so busy trying to make sure the next thing goes right that we can't just be here now and live life. All the while, death is watching our footsteps. Don't you want to live before death comes? You're probably not going to get a warning. Very few people are told when they're going to die. Almost everybody just takes a breath and doesn't know they didn't take another.

So start using every day to let go of that scared part of you that won't let you live life fully. Since you know you're going to die, be willing to say what needs to be said and do what needs to be done. Be willing to be fully present without being afraid of what will happen in the next moment. That's how people live when they face death. You get to do that too, because you are facing death every moment.

Learn to live as though you are facing death at all times, and you'll become bolder and more open. If you live life fully, you won't have any last wishes. You will have lived them every moment. Only then will you have fully experienced life and released the part of you that is afraid of living. There is no reason to be afraid of life. And the fear will fade once you understand that the only thing there is to get from life is the growth that comes from experiencing it. Life itself is your career, and your interaction with life is your most meaningful relationship. Everything else you're doing is just focusing on a tiny subset of life in the attempt to give life some meaning. What actually gives life meaning is the willingness to live it. It isn't any particular event; it's the willingness to experience life's events.

What if you knew that the next person you'd see would be the last person you would ever see? You'd be right there soaking it in, experiencing it. It wouldn't matter what they were saying; you'd just enjoy hearing the words because it would be the last conversation you'd ever have. What if you brought that kind of awareness to every conversation? That's what happens when you're told that death is around the corner: you change, life doesn't change. The true seeker commits to live like that every moment and lets nothing stop them. Why should anything stop you? You're just going to die anyway.

If you challenge yourself to live as though it were your last week, your mind may come up with all kinds of suppressed desires. It may start talking about all the things that you've always wanted to do, and you may think you had better go do them. You will soon see that's not the answer. You have to understand that it is your attempt to get special experiences from life that makes you miss the actual experience of life. Life is not something you get; it's something you experience. Life exists with or without you. It has been going on for billions of years. You simply get the honor of seeing a tiny slice of it. If you're busy trying to get something, you will miss the slice you're actually experiencing. Every one of life's experiences is different, and every experience is worth having. Life is not something to waste. It's truly precious. That's why death is such a great teacher. It is death that makes life precious. Look how precious life becomes when you imagine you only have a week left to live. How precious would life be if there was no such thing as death? You'd waste every second of it because you'd figure you'd always have it. It is scarcity that makes things precious. It is scarcity that makes a simple rock become a rare gem.

So death actually gives meaning to life. Death is your friend. Death is your liberator. For God's sake, do not be afraid of death. Try to learn what it's saying to you. The highest way to learn is to take each moment of your life and realize that what matters is to live it fully. If you live each moment completely, you will have a fuller life and you will not have to fear death.

You fear death because you crave life. You fear death because you think there's something to get that you haven't experienced yet. Many people feel that death will take something away from them. The wise person realizes that death is constantly giving them something. Death is giving meaning to your life. You're the one who throws your life away; you waste every second of it. You get in your car, drive from here to there, and you don't see anything. You're not even there. You're busy thinking about what you're going to do next. You're a month ahead of yourself, or even a year. You're not living life; you're living mind. So it is you who throws your life away, not death. Death actually helps you get your life back by making you pay attention to the moment. It makes you say, "My God, I'm going to lose this. I'm going to lose my children. This could be the last time I'll see them. From now on I'm going to pay more attention to them, and to my spouse, and to all my friends and loved ones. I want to get so much more out of life!"

If you are living every experience fully, then death doesn't take anything from you. There's nothing to take because you're already fulfilled. That's why the wise being is always ready to die. It doesn't make any difference when death comes because their experience is already whole and complete. Suppose you loved music more than anything else. You always wanted to hear your favorite classical composition played by your favorite orchestra. That was the dream of your life. Finally, it happens. You're there and you're actually hearing it. It completely fills you. The very first notes lift you to where you needed to go. This shows you that it only takes a moment to become absorbed in a transcendental peace. You really don't need more time before death; what you need is more depth of experience during the time you're given.

That's the way to live each moment of your life. You let it fill you completely. You let it touch you to the depths of your being. There is no moment that can't do that. Even if something terrible happens, view it as just another experience of life. Death has made you a great promise in which you can find deep peace. The promise is that all things are temporal; they are all just passing through time and space. If you have patience, this too will pass.

The wise realize that in the end, life belongs to death. Death is the one who comes in his own time to take life from you. Death is the landlord and you're just the tenant. People say things like, "He's living on borrowed time," or, "He got a new lease on life." From whom did he borrow the time? From death, of course. Death is the one who comes to claim his property because it has always belonged to him. You should have a healthy relationship with death, and it should not be one of fear. Feel grateful to death for giving you another day, another experience, and for creating the scarcity that makes life so precious. If you do this, your life will no longer be yours to waste; it will be yours to appreciate.

Death is an ultimate reality of life. The yogis and saints fully embrace death. St. Paul said, "Oh death, where is thy sting? Oh grave, where is thy victory?" (1 Cor. 15:55). Great beings don't mind speaking of death. Yogis have traditionally gone into graveyards and burning ghats to meditate. They sit there to remind themselves of the frailty of the body and the inevitability of death. Buddhists are taught to contemplate the temporal nature of things. It is all temporal, and death says this to you.

So, instead of getting lost in the normal mental chatter, why not contemplate the temporal nature of life? Why not think about something meaningful? Don't be afraid of death. Let it free you. Let it encourage you to experience life fully. But remember, it's not your life. You should be experiencing the life that's happening to you, not the one you wish was happening. Don't waste a moment of life trying to make other things happen; appreciate the moments you are given. Don't you understand that every minute you're a step closer to death? This is how to live your life. You live it as though you were on the verge of death, because you are.

CHAPTER 18

the secret of the middle way

No discussion of living life as a spiritual path is complete without addressing one of the deepest of all spiritual teachings, the *Tao te Ching*. It discusses that which is very difficult to discuss, that which Lao-tzu called "the Tao" (pronounced: dow). Literally translated, this means "the Way." The Tao is so subtle that one can only talk around its edges, but never actually touch it. In that treatise, the very basis for the principles of all of life is laid down. It is a treatise on the balance of the yin and the yang, the feminine and the masculine, the dark and the light. You could easily read the *Tao te Ching* and never understand a single word, or you could read it and tears could pour from your eyes with every word you read. The question is, do you bring to it the knowledge, the understanding, and the basis for comprehending what it is attempting to express?

Unfortunately, spiritual teachings often mask the essence of truth with mystical words. But this balance, this Tao, is actually very simple. Those who have truly learned the secrets of life recognize these truths without having read anything. If you want to understand the Tao, you must take it very slowly and keep it very simple. Otherwise, you may miss it, though it is right in front of you.

The Secret of the Middle Way

It is best to approach the Tao through some very simple, almost rhetorical questions. For example, is it good for a person to eat sometimes? Yes, obviously it is. Is it good for a person to eat all the time? No, of course not. Somewhere in between, you passed over the Tao. Is it good to fast periodically? Yes. Is it good to never eat? No. The pendulum can swing all the way from gorging yourself to death, to starving yourself to death. Those are the two extremes of the pendulum: the yin and the yang, expansion and contraction, nondoing and doing. Everything has two extremes. Everything has gradations of this pendulum swing. If you go to the extremes, you cannot survive. That's how extreme the extremes are. For example, do you like hot weather? How about 6,000°F? You'd be instantly vaporized. Do you like cold weather? How about absolute zero? The molecules of your body would never move again.

Let's use an example that is a little less extreme. Do you like being close to another person? How about being so close that you're never apart? You eat every meal together, you go everywhere together, and you do everything together. When you talk on the phone, you always use a speakerphone so that both of you can partake in every conversation. You want to be so close that you're the same person. How long do you think that could last?

That's one extreme in human relationships. The other extreme is that you want your own space. You do your own thing. You're independent. You like being separate so that you always have something to share with each other when you're together. How independent are you? Well, you travel separately, you eat separately, and you live in separate houses. At what point are you so separate that no one can figure out if you're having a relationship? You haven't seen each other for years! Both of these extremes will end up the same. Too close, too far away—in either case, you won't be talking to each other before long. Everything has its extremes, its yin and its yang.

Now let's get a little subtler. The 6,000-degree temperature doesn't sound so good, and absolute zero doesn't sound so interesting either. Neither does starving to death, nor eating until you're sick. But that part about being so close to somebody that you're always together may sound pretty nice. You may at least like to give it a shot. If so, it's because your pendulum has been swung in the opposite direction for too long. You've had too much time alone—too many dinners alone, too many movies alone, and too much traveling alone. In other words, your pendulum has swung off-center.

From science we know that if you pull a pendulum thirty degrees to the right, it will swing back until it's thirty degrees to the left. You don't need Lao-tzu to tell you this. All the laws are the same—inner laws and outer laws. The same principles drive everything in this world. If you pull a pendulum out one way, it will swing back just that far the other way. If you've been starving for days, and somebody puts food in front of you, you won't be polite while you're eating. You will shove the food into your mouth like an animal. The degree to which you will act like an animal is the exact degree to which you were starved enough to bring up your animal instincts.

So where is the Tao? The Tao is in the middle. It's the place where there is no energy pushing in either direction. The pendulum has been permitted to come to balance concerning food, relationships, sex, money, doing, not-doing, and everything else. Everything has its yin and yang. The Way is the place in which these forces balance quietly. And indeed, unless you go out of the Way, they will tend to stay in peaceful harmony. If you want to understand the Tao, you must take a closer look at what lies between the two extremes. This is because neither extreme can last. How long can a pendulum stay at one of its outermost positions? It can only remain there for a moment. How long can a pendulum stay at rest? It can remain there forever because there are no forces moving it out of balance. That is the Tao. It is the center. But that does not mean that it stays static and fixed.

We're about to see that it's much more dynamic than that.

First you have to realize that since everything has its yin and yang, everything has its own balance point. It is the harmony of all these balance points, woven together, that forms the Tao. This overall balance maintains its equilibrium as it moves through time and space. Its power is phenomenal. If you want to imagine the power of the Tao, examine how much energy is wasted swinging sideways. Suppose you want to go from point A to point B, but instead of walking there directly, you move from side to side like a sine wave. That would take a long time, and you would waste a lot of energy. In other words, it's not efficient to oscillate around the path. To be efficient, you must center all of your energies on the path. If you do this, the energies that used to be wasted swinging sideways will get pulled into the center. This concentration of energies is used to accomplish the given task much more efficiently. This is the power of the Tao. When you stop swinging between the opposites you'll find that you have far more energy than you ever imagined. That which takes somebody else hours will take you minutes. That which wears out other people will draw very little of your energy. That's the difference between struggling with the opposites versus staying centered in order to get something done.

The Secret of the Middle Way

This principle holds true in every aspect of life. If you are in balance, you eat when it is time to eat, in a way that maintains the health of your body. To do otherwise is to waste energy dealing with the effects of eating too little, eating too much, or eating the wrong foods. It is much more efficient to deal with the body in a balanced manner than to be burdened with the effects of the extremes.

Basically, you waste tremendous energy at the extremes. The more extreme it is, the more it becomes a full-time project. For example, the relationship in which you insist upon being together all the time would be a full-time job. The only way you could have another job is if you both did the same work at the same desk. At the other extreme, if you had no relationship and you were lonely and depressed all the time, you couldn't accomplish much. So again, it takes all your energy to do the extremes. The inefficiency of your actions is determined by how many degrees off-center you are. You will be that much less able to use your energy for living life because you are using it to adjust for the pendulum swings. Extremes are good teachers. When you examine the extremes, it's easy to see the effects of imbalanced behavior patterns.

Let's take the example of a chain-smoker. He always has a cigarette in his mouth, and he's constantly lighting up another. A meaningful percentage of his life is involved in smoking. He's buying cigarettes, lighting cigarettes, and smoking cigarettes. He's also very busy trying to find places where he's allowed to smoke. And since he doesn't like having to go outside to light up, he's joining the committees in favor of allowing smoking in public places. Notice how much of his energy is going into smoking. Now imagine that he decides to quit— not a single cigarette anymore. If a year later you ask him what he did last year, he will tell you that he quit smoking. That was his life for the past year. First he tried the chewing gum, but that didn't really help. Then he tried the patch. When that didn't work, he moved on to hypnotherapy. Because the pendulum was so far to one extreme with his smoking, it had to swing to the opposite extreme in order for him to stop smoking. Both extremes were a tremendous waste of time, energy, and effort that could have gone into more productive aspects of his life.

When you spend your energy trying to maintain the extremes, nothing goes forward. You get stuck in a rut. The more extreme you are, the less forward movement there is. You carve a groove and you get stuck in it. Then there's no energy moving you in the Tao; it's all being spent serving the extremes.

The Secret of the Middle Way

The Way is in the middle because that's the place where the energies are balanced. But how do you stop the pendulum from swinging to the outer edges? Amazingly enough, you do this by leaving it alone. It won't keep swinging to the extremes unless you feed the extremes with energy. Just let the extremes go. Don't participate in them, and the pendulum will naturally come toward the center. As it comes to the center, you will get filled with energy. This is because all the energy that had been wasted is now available to you.

If you choose to center and not participate in the extremes, you will come to know the Tao. You don't grab it; you don't even touch it. It's just what the energy does when it's not being used to swing toward the extremes. It finds its own way to the center of each event that takes place in life and remains quietly in the middle. The Tao is hollow, empty. Like the eye of a hurricane, its power is its emptiness. All things swirl around it, but it is unmoved. The swirl of life draws its energy from the center and the center draws its energy from the swirl of life. All these laws are the same—in weather, in nature, and in every aspect of your life.

As you center by not participating in the swings, the energies will naturally find their balance. You will become much clearer because so much energy is flowing up in you. The experience of being present in each moment will become your natural state. You won't be fixated on certain things or caught up in thoughts about the opposites. As you get clearer, life's events will actually seem to unfold in slow motion. Once this happens, events will no longer seem confusing or overwhelming, no matter what they are.

This is quite different from how most people live. If they're driving a car and somebody cuts them off, they get upset for the next hour, or maybe for the rest of the day. For the being who is in the Tao, events take place and last just as long as they are taking place. That's it. If you're driving and somebody cuts you off, you feel your energy start to pull off-center. You actually feel it in your heart. As you let go, it comes back to center. You don't follow the extremes, so your energy comes back to the current moment. When the next event happens, you're there. You're always there, and that makes you much more capable than the person who is reacting to past imbalances. Almost everyone has a point at which they get out of balance. Once gone, who's minding the store? Who takes care of the energies that unfold while you're not there? Remember, whoever remains present with fixity of purpose comes out on top in the end.

When you move in the Tao, you are always present. Life becomes absolutely simple. In the Tao, it's easy to see what's happening in life—it's unfolding right in front of you. But if you have all kinds of reactions going on inside because you're involved in the extremes, life seems confusing. That's because you're confused, not because life's confusing.

When you stop being confused, everything becomes simple. If you have no preference, if the only thing you want is to remain centered, then life unfolds while you simply feel for the center. There is an invisible thread that passes through everything. All things move quietly through that center balance. That is the Tao. It is really there. It is there in your relationships, in your diet, and in your business activities. It is there in everything. It is the eye of the storm. It is completely at peace.

To give you an idea of what it feels like to be in that center, let's use the example of sailing. We'll begin by going sailing when there's no wind. That's one extreme, and we're not going anywhere. Now let's go sailing when there's tremendous wind but there's no sail. That is the opposite extreme and, again, we're not going anywhere. Sailing is such a good example because there are many forces interacting together. There's the wind, the sail, the rudder, and the tension of the ropes on the sail. There is a tremendous interplay of forces. What happens if the wind is blowing and you hold the sail too loosely? It doesn't work. What if you hold it too tightly? You tip over. To sail properly you must hold it just right. But where is just right? It is in the center point of tautness of the sail against the force of the wind—not too much, and not too little. It's what we call the "sweet spot." Imagine that feeling when the wind hits the sail just right, and you're holding the ropes just right. You take off with a perfect feeling of balance. Then the wind shifts and you adjust to it. You, the wind, the sail, and the water are one. All the forces are in harmony. Should one force shift, the others shift at the same instant. This is what it means to move in the Way.

In the Tao of sailing, the balance point is not static; it's a dynamic equilibrium. You move from balance point to balance point, from center to center. You can't have any concepts or preferences; you have to let the forces move you. In the Way, nothing is personal. You are merely an instrument in the hands of the forces, participating in the harmony of balance. You must reach the point where your whole interest lies in the balance and not in any personal preference for how things should be. It's that way with all of life. The more you can work with the balance, the more you can just sail through life. Effortless action is what happens when you come into the Tao. Life happens, you're there, but you don't make it happen. There is no burden; there is no stress. The forces take care of themselves as you sit in the center. That is the

The Secret of the Middle Way

Tao. It's the most beautiful place in all of life. You can't touch it, but you can be at one with it.

Eventually you will see that in the way of the Tao you're not going to wake up, see what to do, and then go do it. In the Tao, you are blind, and you have to learn how to be blind. You can never see where the Tao is going; you can only be there with it. A blind person walks down a city street with the use of a cane. Let's give that cane a name: it's the seeker of the extremes, it's the feeler of the edges, it's the toucher of the yin and the yang. People who walk with the use of that cane often tap from side to side. They're not trying to find where they should walk; they're trying to find where they shouldn't walk. They're finding the extremes. If you cannot see your way, all you can do is feel for the edges. But if you feel the edges, and don't go there, you will stay in the Way. That's how you live in the Tao.

All the great teachings reveal the way of the center, the way of balance. Constantly look to see if that's where you are living or if you are lost in the extremes. The extremes create their opposites; the wise avoid them. Find the balance in the center and you will live in harmony.

CHAPTER 19

the loving eyes
of god

How can anyone really know anything about God? We have so many teachings, so many concepts, and so many views about God. But they've all been touched by people. In the end, it's amazing how much our ideas about God conform to the different cultures from which they come.

Fortunately, deep within us, there is a direct connection to the Divine. There is a part of our being that is beyond the personal self. You can consciously choose to identify with that part, rather than with the psyche or the body. When you do this, a natural transformation begins to take place within you. Over time, as you observe this transformation, you will see what it's like to be coming toward God. You actually begin to know what it feels like to be moving in the direction of Spirit. The changes you see within you are reflective of the force you're approaching. Just as rain makes you wet and fire makes you warm, so you can know the nature of God by looking into the mirror of your transformed self. This is not a philosophy; it is a direct experience.

Spiritual growth can be experienced just like anything else. You may have experienced a time in your life when you felt a lot of negativity, anger, and resentment. You know how that feels, and you know how you feel toward others when you're feeling that way. You know how your heart feels, and you know what your thoughts and actions are like. You know that space. It's not a philosophy; it's a direct experience.

If you grow past that part of you, over time you will actually drift away from the feelings of tension and anxiety. The entire cloud of lower vibrations will appear further and further away from where you sit inside. The cloud may still be there, but if you don't identify with it or hold onto it, it can no longer hold onto you. As you release the lower vibrations, you naturally stop thinking they're you or that there's anything you have to do about them. As you let go of them, your Spirit drifts upward.

How do you know your Spirit drifts upward? You know the same way you know that you're breathing, the same way you know that your heart beats, and the same way you know that you have thoughts. You're in there and you directly experience it.

What does it mean to drift upward? It's an experience of being drawn further back inside yourself. You're no longer held down to your earthly self, so you begin to feel more spaciousness inside. You feel that there's more of a distance between you and the thoughts and emotions inside of you. You drift back, and then in and up.

How does it feel when you drift up? You don't feel as much anger, fear, or self-consciousness. You don't feel resentment toward people. You don't close or get tight as often. Things still happen that you don't want to happen, but they don't seem to touch you as much. They can't reach back to where you are because you've drifted behind the part of you that reacts to things. These are actual experiences, not merely something you were told about. It's just what naturally happens when you let go of the lower vibrations of your being. You drift in and up to the deeper vibrations.

Where are you going? Even if you have no basis for understanding what is happening to you, you are still having the undeniable experience of going somewhere. What you begin to feel is that you're going into your spiritual being. As you associate less with the physical and psychological parts of your being, you begin to identify more with the flow of pure energy.

What does it feel like to identify more with Spirit than with form? You used to walk around feeling anxiety and tension; now you walk around feeling love. You just feel love for no reason. Your backdrop is love. Your backdrop is openness, beauty, and appreciation. You don't have to make yourself feel that way; that is how Spirit feels. If you were asked how the body normally feels, you might say that it's generally uncomfortable about one thing or another. How about the psyche? If you were being totally honest, you'd probably say that it's generally full of complaints and fears. Well, how does Spirit normally feel? The truth is, it always feels good. It always feels high. It always feels open and light.

Because of this, you naturally begin to center more and more on the spiritual part of your being. You do this not by reaching for Spirit, but by letting go of the rest. There really is no other way. The personal self cannot touch Spirit; you must release the personal self. As you release it, you drift back. As you go further back, you get higher. You get higher in vibration and higher in the amount of love and lightness that you feel. You just begin to soar. This happens in an ever-increasing, continuous progression.

As you let go and willingly release the physical, emotional, and mental aspects of your being, Spirit becomes your state. You don't claim to understand what is happening to you; you just know that as you go further and further back, it gets more and more beautiful. You naturally begin to experience the vibrations that were described by the great saints and sages of different traditions. You realize that you, too, can have deep spiritual experiences and be "...in the Spirit on the Lord's Day" (Rev. 1:10).

But ultimately, how do you really know anything about God? How can you ever know about what is beyond you? You know because those who have gone beyond have come back and said that the Spirit you're experiencing is the doorway to God. When they let go of the lower aspects of their being, they experienced just what you're experiencing. They felt tremendous love, Spirit, and light waking up inside of them. They felt that nothing could come in through their senses that was higher than what was already going on inside. They drifted further and further back and got higher and higher. Then one day, all of a sudden, they weren't there. There was no sense of "I" anymore. There was no sense of a separateness experiencing the love and light. There was only the ultimate expansiveness of their sense of Self merging into the love and light, like a single drop of water merging into the ocean.

When the drop of consciousness that knows itself as an individual drifts back far enough, it becomes like the drop that falls into the ocean. The Atman (Soul) falls into the Paramatman (Supreme Soul). The individual consciousness falls into the Universal Oneness. And that's it.

When that happens, people say interesting things like, "I and my Father are one" (John 10:30) and "… the words that I speak unto you I speak not of myself: but the Father that dwelleth in me, he doeth the works" (John 14:10).

They all spoke like that. They said they had merged and that there was no differentiation within the Universal

The Loving Eyes of God

Oneness of God. The drop of consciousness, which is individual Spirit, is like a ray of light emanating from the sun. The individual ray is really no different from the sun. When consciousness stops identifying itself as the ray, it comes to know itself as the sun. Beings have merged into that state.

In the mystical Gospel of John, Christ says, "That they all may be one; as thou, Father, art in me, and I in thee, that they also may be one in us … I in them, and thou in me, that they may be made perfect in one…" (John 17:21-23). So it was taught in the Hindu Vedas; so it was taught in the Jewish Kabbalah; so it was written by the great Sufi mystic poets; and so it was taught in all the great religious traditions of all time. Such a state exists; one can merge into the Universal Absolute. One can merge into God.

This is how you know something about God. You become one with Him. Ultimately, the only way to know about God is by letting your being merge into The Being, and then seeing what happens to you. This is universal consciousness, and the qualities of the beings who have attained this deep state are similar in every religion.

What happens to one who walks this path toward God? What transformations do they go through along the way? To understand this, imagine what would happen if you started feeling tremendous love for all creatures, for every plant, for every animal, and for all the beauties of nature. Imagine if every child seemed like your own, and every person you saw looked like a beautiful flower, with its own color, its own expression, shape, and sounds. As you went deeper and deeper, you would start noticing a phenomenal thing—you are no longer judging. The process of judging has simply stopped. There is just appreciating and honoring. Where there used to be judging, there is now respecting, loving, and cherishing. To differentiate is to judge. To see, to experience, and to honor is to participate in life instead of standing back and judging it.

When you walk through a beautiful botanical garden, you feel open and light. You feel love. You see beauty. You don't judge the shape and placement of every leaf. The leaves are of all sizes and shapes and they face every-which-way. That's what makes them beautiful. What if you felt that way about people? What if they didn't all have to dress the same, believe the same, or behave the same? What if they were like the flowers, and however they happened to be seemed beautiful to you?

If that happened, you'd get a glimpse of God. That's the best way to know God. Watch what happens to you as you get closer to Him. It's really the only way you can know anything about God. If you try to read about God in a book, you'll find five other books that say the opposite. Better yet, you'll find five interpretations of the same book. Somebody writes something and somebody else gets a Ph.D. proving it wrong. If you move your search for God down to the mental level, somebody will dispute it. It's all part of the mind game.

You can't know God that way. It must come from actual experience. That's what happens to you when you meditate. That's what happens when you let go of your lower self. You drift into Spirit, and as you drift into Spirit, these transformations take place within you. All you have to do is notice them, and you will start to notice the tendency toward the qualities of the Divine. The further back you go, the more you will see these natural qualities unfolding inside of you. Each step along the way, you get a clearer glimpse of what it must be like to sit in that Divine State.

There are those who know of the existence of the Divine Force. They've had enough direct inner experience to know that Divine Consciousness is a reality. They have seen glimpses of a force that is omniscient, omnipresent, and omnipotent; a force that is aware of all things at all times, equally. It is universally conscious.

What does creation look like from that Divine State? What have they seen, those who have gone beyond and looked through the eyes of God? They see that there is no judging. Judging faded away long ago. There's just more beauty to see. Such a being feels, "Now I can see all the flowers at once. Now I can experience what each of my children and all of my diversity is doing. Now I can feel more love, more compassion, more understanding, and more admiration for all the different expressions and actions of my creation." That is what it looks like to a saint. And a true saint dwells with God.

What if it is really true that God is not judging? What if God is loving? We all know that true love doesn't judge. Love sees nothing but beauty in its beloved. There is no impurity. There is no possibility of impurity. No matter what it beholds, it's all beautiful. That is how true love sees. That is what it looks like through the eyes of love. So if God is love, what must it look like through those eyes—the eyes that are filled with infinite love and unconditional compassion?

If you've ever really loved anybody, then you know what true love means. It means that you love them more than you love yourself. If you truly love someone, your love sees past their humanness. It embraces their whole being, including past wrongs and current shortcomings. It is like the unconditional love of a mother. A mother devotes every moment of her life to a child who is physically or mentally challenged. She thinks the child is beautiful. She doesn't focus on the shortcomings; in fact, she doesn't even see them as shortcomings.

The Loving Eyes of God

What if that is how God looks upon His creation? Then you've lost out if you've been told otherwise. Instead of being encouraged to feel completely protected, loved, honored, and respected by the Divine Force, you've been taught that you're being judged. Because you've been taught that, you feel guilt and fear. But guilt and fear do not open your connection to the Divine; they only serve to close your heart. The reality is that God's way is love, and you can see this for yourself. If, for even one moment, you can look at someone with the eyes of true love, you'll know those eyes are not yours. Your eyes could never look with that amount of love. Your eyes could never be that unconditional. Your eyes could never, even in a million years, see only beauty and total perfection in your beloved. Those are the eyes of God looking down through you.

When the hand of God reaches out to give through you, there's nothing you wouldn't give. You would give your last breath and never even think about it. It wouldn't even cross your mind to hold back. You would give anything and everything for your beloved. When you feel love this deeply, you feel that it is coming from something greater than you. It is transcendental love. It is divine, unconditional, selfless love. The masters spoke of that love. The ones who went beyond said it's the state you attain when you drift into Spirit. That is how

Spirit looks upon its creation. That is what you should be taught. No matter what you do, and no matter what you've done, you will always be loved by Him.

When Christ told the story of the prodigal son to his disciples, he spoke of one son who had gone away and squandered all his wealth. Yet when he came home for help, his father treated him better than the son who had stayed home and worked. Christ explained that this was because one son had always been home, but the prodigal son had been lost, and the father had missed him. There was no judging—only loving (Luke 15:11-32).

Christ also said, "He that is without sin among you, let him first cast a stone…" (John 8:7). What did he teach? What did he say? How did he look upon this world? He taught completely selfless, compassionate love. He hung on the cross next to thieves and robbers, and when a thief asked to be remembered, Christ said that he would share that day in heaven with him (Luke 23:39-43). What were his first words upon the cross? "Father, forgive them; for they know not what they do" (Luke 23:34). That is the love of a mother. That's how a mother talks about her child. The level of love and compassion is so deep that the child can do no wrong. If a mother can attain to selfless love, then what about God, the creator of love?

The Loving Eyes of God

Do you want to know how God looks upon this world? Do you want to know how He feels about different kinds of people? Then look at the sun. Does the sun shine more brightly on a saint than on anyone else? Is the air more available to the saint? Does the rain fall on one neighbor's trees more than another's?

You can turn your eyes from the sun's light and live in darkness for a hundred years. If you then turn them toward the light, the light is still there. It is there for you just the same as for the person who has enjoyed its brilliance for a hundred years. All of nature is like this. The fruit on the tree willingly gives itself to everyone. Do any of the forces of nature differentiate? Does anything in God's creation, other than the human mind, actually pass judgment? Nature just gives and gives to whoever will receive. Should you choose not to receive, it doesn't punish you. You punish yourself because you choose not to receive. If you say to the light, "I will not look at you. I'm going to live in darkness," the light just keeps shining. If you say to God, "I don't believe in you and want nothing to do with you," creation continues to sustain you.

Your relationship with God is the same as your relationship with the sun. If you hid from the sun for years and then chose to come out of your darkness, the sun would still be shining as if you had never left. You don't need to apologize. You just pick your head up and look at the sun. It's the same way when you decide to turn toward God—you just do it. If, instead, you allow guilt and shame to interfere, that's just your ego blocking the Divine Force. You can't offend the Divine One; its very nature is light, love, compassion, protection, and giving. You can't make it stop loving you. It's just like the sun. You can't make the sun stop shining on you; you can only choose not to look at it. The moment you look, you'll see it's there.

As you drift back into Spirit, you will see that those are the eyes that look out upon this world. That is the heart that shines down upon everything and everyone. Through those eyes, the most wretched of creatures looks beautiful. That's the part that no one understands. People say that God cries when He looks at this earth. The saint sees that God goes into ecstasy when He looks upon this earth, under all conditions, and at all times. Ecstasy is the only thing God knows. God's nature is eternal, conscious bliss. No matter what you've done, you're not going to be the one thing that ruins it.

The beauty is that you can experience this ecstasy. And when you begin to feel this joy, that's when you'll know God's nature. Then nobody will upset or disappoint you. Nothing will create a problem. It will all appear as part of the beautiful dance of creation unfolding before you. Your natural state will get higher and higher. You'll feel love instead of shame. Instead of being unwilling to lift your eyes to the Divine because of what you've said or done, you'll see the Divine as a place of unconditional refuge.

Contemplate this, and let go of the idea of a judgmental God. You have a loving God. In truth, you have love itself for a God. And love cannot do other than love. Your God is in ecstasy and there's nothing you can do about it. And if God is in ecstasy, I wonder what He sees when He looks at you?

references

Freud, Sigmund. 1927. *The Ego and the Id*. Authorized translation by Joan Riviere. London: Leonard & Virginia Woolf at the Hogarth Press, and the Institute of Psycho-Analysis.

Holy Bible: King James Version. Grand Rapids, MI: Zondervan.

Maharshi, Ramana. 1972. *The Spiritual Teachings of Ramana Maharshi*. Copyright 1972 by Sri Ramanasramam. Biographical sketch and glossary copyright 1998 Shambhala Publications, Inc. Boston: Shambhala Publications, Inc.

Merriam-Webster. 2003. *Merriam-Webster's Collegiate Dictionary*. 11th ed. Springfield, MA: Merriam-Webster.

Microsoft Encarta Dictionary by Microsoft. Accessed April 17, 2007. http://encarta.msn.com/encnet/features/dictionary/dictionaryhome.aspx.

Plato. 1998 edition. *Republic*. Translated with an introduction and notes by Robin Waterfield. New York: Oxford University Press, Inc.

Yamamoto, Kosho. 1973 edition. *The Mahaparinirvana Sutra*. Translated from the Chinese of Kumarajiva. *The Karin Buddhological Series No. 5*. Yamaguchi-ken, Japan: Karinbunko.

The Institute of Noetic Sciences

The Institute of Noetic Sciences (IONS) is a research center and direct-experience lab specializing in the intersection of science and profound human experience.

For centuries, the power of science has unlocked the mysteries of the natural world and driven human innovation. As Dr. Edgar Mitchell returned to Earth from his moonwalk on Apollo 14, he had a profound transcendence experience that led him to establish IONS in 1973. He understood that by applying the scientific rigor used in his explorations of outer space, we could better understand the mysteries of inner space—the space in which he felt an undeniable sense of interconnection and oneness. The mission of IONS is to reveal the interconnected nature of reality through scientific exploration and personal discovery, creating a more compassionate, thriving, and sustainable world.

At IONS, we are inspired by the power of science to explain phenomena not previously understood, harnessing the best of the rational mind to make advances that further our knowledge and deepen our knowing. For over four decades, IONS has provided a safe harbor for scientists and scholars to pursue research into frontier questions related to the nature of consciousness, and for healers and educators to work with emerging ideas. From our scientific exploration, we design experiential programs for personal discovery that allow each of us to access more of our human capacities and the fullness of our humanity.

Today, IONS continues to forge new frontiers in consciousness research and experiential education, developing training programs for youth, adults, elders, and professionals; all on a majestic 197-acre retreat center in Petaluma, CA, one hour north of San Francisco, CA.

IONS INSTITUTE OF NOETIC SCIENCES   **Learn more and join us at noetic.org**

About the Author

MICHAEL A. SINGER is author of the #1 *New York Times* bestseller, *The Untethered Soul*, and the *New York Times* bestseller, *The Surrender Experiment*, which have both been published worldwide. He had a deep inner awakening in 1971 while working on his doctorate in economics, and went into seclusion to focus on yoga and meditation. In 1975, he founded Temple of the Universe, a now long-established yoga and meditation center where people of any religion or set of beliefs can come together to experience inner peace. He is also creator of a leading-edge software package that transformed the medical practice management industry, and founding CEO of a billion-dollar public company whose achievements are archived in the Smithsonian Institution. Along with his more than four decades of spiritual teaching, Singer has made major contributions in the areas of business, education, health care, and environmental protection. He previously authored two books on the integration of Eastern and Western philosophy: *The Search for Truth* and *Three Essays on Universal Law*.

Visit www.untetheredsoul.com for more information.

» Hear Michael A. Singer read from *The Untethered Soul* at: newharbinger.com/tus
» Watch an in-depth INTERVIEW with Michael A. Singer at: bit.ly/tusinterview
» Watch the BOOK TRAILER at: bit.ly/tustrailer
» Find AUDIO TALKS by Michael A. Singer at: store.untetheredsoul.com

Start a group discussion with
The Untethered Soul
Reading Group Guide,
available for free download at
www.newharbinger.com/untetheredguide.